D0854899

Living Through the Great Depression

EXPLORING CULTURAL HISTORY

Tracy Brown Collins, *Book Editor*

Bruce Glassman, *Vice President*
Bonnie Szumski, *Publisher*
Helen Cothran, *Managing Editor*

GREENHAVEN
PRESS ®

THOMSON
GALE

San Diego • Detroit • New York • San Francisco • Cleveland
New Haven, Conn. • Waterville, Maine • London • Munich

For more information, contact
Greenhaven Press
27500 Drake Rd.
Farmington Hills, MI 48331-3535
Or you can visit our Internet site at http://www.gale.com

LIBRARY OF CONGRESS CATALOGING-IN-PUBLICATION DATA
Living through the Great Depression / Tracy Brown Collins, book editor.
    p. cm. — (Exploring cultural history)
Includes bibliographical references and index.
ISBN 0-7377-2096-4 (lib. : alk. paper)
    1. United States—History—1933–1945—Sources. 2. Depressions—1929—
United States—Sources. 3. United States—Social conditions—1933–1945—
Sources. 4. United States—Social life and customs—1918–1945—Sources.
5. Popular culture—United States—History—Twentieth century—Sources.
I. Collins, Tracy Brown, 1972– . II. Series.
E806.L6 2004
973.91'6—dc22   2003056833

Contents

Chapter 4: Communities and Support

Foreword

Too often, history books and teachers place an overemphasis on events and dates. Students learn that key births, battles, revolutions, coronations, and assassinations occurred in certain years. But when many centuries separate these happenings from the modern world, they can seem distant, disconnected, even irrelevant.

The reality is that today's society is *not* disconnected from the societies that preceded it. In fact, modern culture is a sort of melting pot of various aspects of life in past cultures. Over the course of centuries and millennia, one culture passed on some of its traditions, in the form of customs, habits, ideas, and beliefs, to another, which modified and built on them to fit its own needs. That culture then passed on its own version of the traditions to later cultures, including today's. Pieces of everyday life in past cultures survive in our own lives, therefore. And it is often these morsels of tradition, these survivals of tried and true past experience, that people most cherish, take comfort in, and look to for guidance. As the great English scholar and archaeologist Sir Leonard Woolley put it, "We cannot divorce ourselves from our past. We are always conscious of precedents . . . and we let experience shape our views and actions."

Thus, for example, Americans and the inhabitants of a number of other modern nations can pride themselves on living by the rule of law, educating their children in formal schools, expressing themselves in literature and art, and following the moral precepts of various religions and philosophies. Yet modern society did not invent the laws, schools, literature, art, religions, and philosophies that pervade it; rather, it inherited these things from previous cultures. "Time, the great destroyer, is also the great preserver," the late, noted thinker Herbert J. Muller once observed. "It has preserved . . . the immense accumulation of products, skills, styles, customs, institutions, and ideas that make the man on the American street indebted to all the peoples of history, including some who never saw a street." In this way, ancient Mesopotamia gave the world its first cities and literature; ancient Egypt, large-scale architecture; ancient Israel, the formative concepts of Judaism,

Christianity, and Islam; ancient Greece, democracy, the theater, Olympic sports, and magnificent ceramics; ancient China, gunpowder and exotic fabrics; ancient Rome and medieval England, their pioneering legal systems; Renaissance Italy, great painting and sculpture; Elizabethan England, the birth of modern drama; and colonial America, the formative environments of the founders of the United States, the most powerful and prosperous nation in world history. Only by looking back on those peoples and how they lived can modern society understand its roots.

Not all the products of cultural history have been so constructive, however. Most ancient Greeks severely restricted the civil rights and daily lives of women, for instance; the Romans kept and abused large numbers of slaves, as did many Americans in the years preceding the Civil War; and Nazi Germany and the Soviet Union curbed or suppressed freedom of speech, assembly, and religion. Examining these negative aspects of life in various past cultures helps to expose the origins of many of the social problems that exist today; it also reminds us of the ever-present potential for people to make mistakes and pursue misguided or destructive social and economic policies.

The books in the Greenhaven Press Exploring Cultural History series provide readers with the major highlights of life in human cultures from ancient times to the present. The family, home life, food and drink, women's duties and rights, childhood and education, arts and leisure, literacy and literature, roads and means of communications, slavery, religious beliefs, and more are examined in essays grouped by theme. The essays in each volume have been chosen for their readability and edited to manageable lengths. Many are primary sources. These original voices from a past culture echo through the corridors of time and give the volume a strong feeling of immediacy and authenticity. The other essays are by historians and other modern scholars who specialize in the culture in question. An annotated table of contents, chronology, and extensive bibliography broken down by theme add clarity and context. Thus, each volume in the Greenhaven Press Exploring Cultural History series opens a unique window through which readers can gaze into a distant time and place and eavesdrop on life in a long vanished culture.

Introduction

The 1920s were a prosperous time in America. Industry was booming—factories produced goods such as cars and radios at rates not seen before, and it was said that between 1919 and 1929 the productivity rate of a single worker had increased more than 30 percent. America's economy was very top-heavy during the 1920s, however, with the top 1 percent of the population owning approximately 40 percent of the nation's wealth. Many of America's millionaires owed their wealth in various degrees to the stock market frenzy of the 1920s. Because the government did not police the stock market, practices of manipulating it for profit were common, both by businesses and individuals.

While industry boomed during the twenties, agriculture waned. American farmers had prospered during World War I, thanks to demand for their crops overseas. With their boosted incomes, farmers were able to purchase machinery to replace animals and use what had been pasture land to plant still more crops. But the end of the war meant the end of the additional demand for crops, and crop values dropped. The value of farmland also fell 30 to 40 percent between 1920 and 1929.

In 1929 the unemployment rate in America was 3.2 percent. By 1930 it had risen to 8.7 percent. By 1932, the worst year of the Depression, it had risen to a staggering 25.2 percent. Forty percent of the banks in America in 1929 also had collapsed by 1932.

Unemployment led to evictions. In Detroit, home to the previously prosperous automobile industry, more than 220,000 people were out of work in 1931. Landlords began evicting families who could no longer afford their rents. Emergency camps were set up for homeless families in city parks. In rural areas, poverty was further increased when drought hit Oklahoma, Texas, and Arkansas in 1931. In 1932, on average, one thousand families a week lost their farms to banks that owned the titles to the farms. This caused a mass migration to California of farmers in search of work.

The effects of the Depression were devastating. That the Depression went on for so long made it even more so. At the time, many blamed the Hoover administration's response to the Depression for its severity and length. In fact, the government reacted to this depression as it had always done in previous depressions, by relying on local governments to organize charities and aid programs rather than to organize federal aid. The shift in thinking regarding the government's role in a depression and in helping individuals in need was one major outcome of the Great Depression.

The Hoover Years

From the end of the Civil War to the start of the 1930s, most Americans were committed to ideas of small government and big business. Americans, obsessed with procuring wealth throughout the 1920s—there were more millionaires in America during this decade than ever before—did not believe that government had a right to interfere in the wealth or business practices of the private sector. It was in this environment that Herbert Hoover became president in 1928.

Hoover was an optimistic president who believed Americans only had to be more confident to fight off an economic depression. When the economy first began to slide, Hoover advised businesses not to lower wages, but this only led to layoffs. He also believed that nations could overcome all adversities through the cooperation and hard work of every individual. These were attitudes that were popular when he was elected, but which would later make him one of the most disliked presidents in history.

As unemployment and poverty rose, Hoover encouraged city and state governments to organize private charities to help combat the Depression, and local governments and citizens took Hoover's mandate seriously. In 1931, for example, Boston mayor James Michael Curley asked that all but the very lowest paid Bostonians donate a day's wage to an emergency relief fund. The mayor gave approximately $4,000 of his own money, and by 1932 his program had raised $3 million. As unemployment increased, however, it became apparent that such private efforts could not alleviate the protracted struggle that the Depression represented.

But Hoover did not budge on the idea that individuals and grassroots charities could solve the problem. He did not believe federal relief was the answer—indeed, he did not think it was fitting of the character of most Americans. Although Hoover's government did in fact expand its role more than any previous administration, he still believed that the government had a responsibility to intervene in the private sector only as much as was necessary.

For example, Hoover approved the spending of $45 million to feed starving cattle in Arkansas during the drought in 1930, but he refused to grant $25 million to feed the farmers themselves. Adhering to the adage, "Give a man a fish and he eats for one day, teach a man to fish and he eats for a lifetime," Hoover did not want Americans to become reliant on government aid. Spending money on feeding cattle enabled the farmers to work for themselves. Feeding them directly did not.

Some people remained in the upper class and maintained their ideas of individualism, although in the early 1930s and throughout the Depression many in the middle class now found themselves unemployed, homeless, and hungry. Suddenly, America's large middle class could relate far better to the poorer class than to the upper one, and this is when Americans' philosophy on the role of government began to change.

People began to blame Hoover's policies for the Depression. In 1931 *Time* magazine called him the President Reject. A widely distributed photograph of Hoover feeding his dog on the White House lawn angered the poor who could not afford to feed their families, let alone pets. Shantytowns where the homeless lived in cardboard boxes were called "Hoovervilles." People shoved newspapers in their pockets to try to keep warm and called them "Hoover blankets." These and other examples of such terminology indicate how much the American attitude toward their government and its responsibility to its people had changed. With the 1932 election approaching, Hoover had become one of the most hated men in America.

Americans Seek a New Kind of Leadership

During his acceptance speech at the Democratic Convention during the 1932 primary election, Franklin D. Roosevelt pledged "a new deal for the American people." He was immediately popular with the working and lower classes who looked on him as their one last hope. It was not just his politics—he gave few concrete strategies for reducing unemployment during his campaign—but his style that people immediately trusted. Roosevelt defeated Hoover in the election, and when he told Americans during his inaugural address that they had nothing to fear but "fear itself," they believed him. And the pressure was on to keep his comforting promises.

Bank panics, in which people who lost confidence in their banks rushed to withdraw all of their funds, had been common since the start of the Depression. In March 1932 another bank panic occurred, and one of Roosevelt's first actions as president was to impose a four-day bank holiday, which closed the banks and hence stopped people from withdrawing all of their money in panic. Only banks that could prove solvent reopened. This action went against the previously held belief that the government had no place interfering in such matters. He also passed the Emergency Banking Relief Act, which imposed mandatory governmental inspections of federal banks and insured bank deposits.

Having tackled the banking problem, the president focused on battling unemployment. That same March, Roosevelt proposed the Civilian Conservation Corps (CCC), a government organization to provide jobs for able-bodied, unmarried men. In 1935 Roosevelt launched the Works Progress Administration (WPA) which provided jobs that offered a livable wage. The WPA consisted of a number of programs that included jobs for unemployed artists and writers. The WPA consisted of the Federal Art Project, the Federal Music Project, the Federal Theatre Project, the Federal Writers' Project, and the Historical Records Survey.

People's confidence in Roosevelt was increased by the ways in which he communicated with the American people. Unlike Hoover, Roosevelt was not intimidated by the press. Early on in his presidency he announced that he wanted to meet with the press as often as possible and that he would give two press conferences a week. The president and the first lady, Eleanor, both encouraged the American people to write to them and let them know their concerns and opinions. Beginning in 1933 Roosevelt addressed the nation in a warm, personal manner during Sunday night radio broadcasts know as Fireside Chats.

American Society Is Changed: The Depression's Legacy

Roosevelt's New Deal policies helped restore America's confidence. His presidency also represented a major shift in how

Americans perceived the role of government. It took the scope and stubborn protractedness of the Great Depression to bring about this change in perception.

However, the New Deal did not on its own pull America out of its depression. In 1939 the unemployment rate was still at 17.2 percent. From 1939 until America joined the war in 1941, manufacturing jumped 50 percent, putting millions back to work. Although it was the start of World War II that eventually brought America out of the Depression, many think Roosevelt had been the leader America needed during the crisis, and he was beloved by many. Roosevelt died in April 1945, during his fourth consecutive term as president.

Conclusion

The Great Depression has been called the second worst disaster America has seen—second only to the Civil War. Its severity and persistence changed the priorities of Americans. While procuring wealth had been a central value of the 1920s, people who had lost nearly everything were now more concerned with securing what they had. The Depression also changed how Americans felt about the type of government they needed. Roosevelt and his New Deal programs represented a significant shift in the government's role in people's lives that continues today.

People and Private Life

CHAPTER
1

Chapter Preface

The Great Depression brought insecurity into the lives of those who lived through it. People who had, throughout the previous decade, been able to rely on steady work, a place to live, and marriage and children now had to change their expectations.

Poverty forced many children who wanted to attend school and perhaps go on to college to no longer have such ambitions. Men and women who lost their jobs were cast from secure, skilled work into a desperate search for any kind of work for any kind of wage. They had to rethink plans they had for marriage and children, both because the Depression deprived people of the money for such things and because people were uprooted so frequently in order to look for work that it prevented them from establishing stable relationships.

The dramatic change in the security of American life led to the creation of new government programs that would help people find work and restore their confidence.

Love and Marriage During the Great Depression

Deb Mulvey

Many marriages suffered under the strain of the Great Depression. Some men were forced to leave their families in search of work. Others felt the emotional anguish of being unable to provide for their wives and children. Numerous single people who were struggling economically decided against marriage during the Depression years, not wanting the burden of a spouse and children. This, however, did not prevent single people from engaging in sexual activity, and abortion rates rose as marriage rates declined. But many did go ahead with their marriage plans. The following vignettes, taken from *We Had Everything but Money*, a collection of interviews and anecdotes edited by Deb Mulvey about life during the Great Depression, describes courtships, proposals, weddings, and receptions during the period.

Most Weddings Were Simple, Inexpensive

Weddings were seldom elaborate during the 1930s. There were no bachelor parties, rehearsal dinners or expensive wedding dresses.

Most couples were married in a private ceremony before a judge or clergyman, with one person to "stand up" with them as an attendant.

It was always a great day when one of our Bohemian-Polish neighbors got married, as their celebrations sometimes lasted as long as 3 days! Everyone got together, brought food and danced. Sometimes the male guests paid a dollar—*a whole dollar!*—to dance with the bride.

But most of us celebrated with a shivaree. The ladies would bring food and shower gifts. My own gifts included 13 table-cloths! When my husband and I opened a restaurant years later, we used those cherished cloths many times for special occasions.

—*Marcia D. Bloomfield*
Adams, Wisconsin

"An Illinois Farm Girl Won My Heart"

In the spring of 1937 I was starting to think about settling down, but most of the girls in my Michigan hometown were either already married or had moved to the city to look for jobs. I asked my cousin's wife if she knew any girls back in her hometown in southern Illinois.

"Why, yes," she said. "I know a nice farm girl you might like."

I wrote a letter of introduction, which the girl answered politely. We corresponded until September, and then I decided we should meet in person so I traveled 550 miles to her home.

I was met at the door by a very pretty young lady and her family, and we spent several days getting better acquainted. It didn't take long to realize I wanted her to be my wife. After I returned home, I wrote her a letter asking her to marry me.

The night before I expected her answer, I dreamed a rattlesnake bit me! With such a bad omen, I expected the worst, and when her letter arrived I kept it in my pocket all day, afraid to open it. When I finally did, my hunch was correct. "Stop wasting your paper," she wrote. "I am not interested."

I courted other girls, but I never got that Illinois farm girl out of my mind. Three years later, I was walking past the drugstore and saw a Valentine's Day display. Suddenly, I knew just what to do. I bought her a 5¢ valentine with a little bear on it and the words: "I couldn't bear it if you won't be my valentine."

To my delight, she replied that if I was still interested in her after all that time, she'd be happy to correspond again. I went to visit her that May, and we were married in September.

My wife turned out to be a rare jewel, and we raised two fine children. In 1991 we celebrated our 51st anniversary and have our sights set on many more.

—*Harry J. Steiner*
Bellaire, Michigan

Couple Met on Scavenger Hunt

Whenever someone asks my husband how we met, he always says, "I found her on a scavenger hunt!"

It was 1937, and we were freshmen at a small college in Iowa. The scavenger hunt was organized to help the new students get acquainted, and it certainly worked for us! My future husband and I were paired off and instructed to request a clerical collar from the minister. We got the collar, and we were married 5 years later.

—*Veda Wilson Fatka*
Muskegon, Michigan

Ride Became Lifelong Journey

When we were in high school, most of us didn't have cars, so we rode our bicycles around in the evenings. One night I boldly asked the prettiest girl in the neighborhood if she'd like to take a ride with me. She accepted, and we've been riding through life together ever since!

—*John Bedner*
Colonia, New Jersey

Pen Pals Had "Write Stuff"

I worked in our small town's telephone office, and one night when business was slow, a co-worker and I found a magazine with letters from people looking for pen pals. We'd never seen that before and thought it would be fun to send in letters of our own. I wasn't looking for a boyfriend; I was already engaged. I was just curious to see what would happen!

I got many responses, including one from a lonely young man who lived about 3 hours away. We exchanged snapshots and I told him I was engaged. "When you get married," he wrote, "I'll send you a high chair."

He didn't need to, though. Not long after that, I decided marriage wasn't for me and broke off my engagement.

When it came time for my vacation, my sister and I went to a beach town with an aunt and uncle. I was walking on the boardwalk with a young man I'd met there, and got sand in my shoes. As he knelt down to clean my shoes, he muttered, "If that guy doesn't stop following us, I'll fix him!"

I hadn't noticed anyone following us, so I turned to look.

When my companion pointed, I saw none other than the man who'd promised to send me a high chair!

My pen pal and I spent the last few days of my vacation together, and I was sorry when it was time to leave. As my sister and I were returning home, she handed me a tin egg my pen pal and I had won at the penny arcade. "Your friend asked me to give this to you," she said.

When I opened it, I found a note inside that said: "Why don't we get married?" Two weeks later, we did! And he bought me the high chair, too!

—*Evelyn Sudduth*
Fresno, California

Caroling Brought Couple Together

In December 1934 our youth group was going Christmas caroling and gathered at the church to load up in cars. One girl had brought a visitor, a young man named Robert Miller. As we piled into the cars, it turned out I had to sit on Robert's lap! Fifty-seven years later, he still claims I "made an impression" on him.

—*Mrs. Robert F. Miller*
Fresno, Ohio

She "Roped" Her Husband—Literally!

My husband and I met on horseback! My family lived on a ranch along the White River in South Dakota, and my brother and I broke horses to make our spending money. When I was 15, we heard new neighbors had moved in about 2 miles up the river with a son around my age.

One evening I rode my horse to the river to bring the milk cows home, and I heard a noise in the bushes. When I moved closer to check it out, a young man, also on horseback, came tearing out and rode upriver as fast as he could!

Well, my horse was pretty fast, too, so I took off after him. I not only caught him—I roped him! He was embarrassed, but I couldn't help noticing how cute he was. Five years later I married that neighbor boy, and he became a good roper himself. In fact, he won many roping events in local rodeos.

—*Frances Jensen*
Kimball, South Dakota

Valentines Lasted a Lifetime

I met my husband-to-be at a neighborhood Easter egg hunt. I was 4 and he was 6. I had left my basket unattended for a moment, and when I returned, the eggs were gone. When I began to cry, a handsome little blond boy comforted me and gave me his eggs!

When I started school in 1933, this same boy sent me the first of many valentines, a big lacy heart that said, "Be my valentine." We were together all through grade school and high school and never dated anyone else.

From 1933 until my husband's death, he never failed to give me a valentine every February 14. We were married 25 years, but in my heart we had been together for 39—from the moment he gave me that first valentine.

—*Jeanette D. Blount*
Paris, Kentucky

Trip to Heal the Body Also Opened His Heart

I contracted tuberculosis as a youth, and even after I recovered, the Indiana winters were hard on me. In an effort to regain my health, I moved to Arizona. Money was scarce, so I rode the bus only part of the way and hitchhiked for the rest of the trip.

While attending church in Tucson, I met a wonderful girl, and we fell in love and decided to marry. My health improved, but there were no jobs for me in Tucson, so I returned to Indiana to look for work. Employment was all but impossible to find; the only jobs I could get were temporary ones. Without steady work, there was no way Emma and I could be married.

Since we couldn't be together, Emma and I kept our love alive by writing to each other every day. Hundreds of letters passed between Indiana and Arizona as I kept searching for work.

Finally, after Emma and I had been separated for 16 months, I became assistant manager of the F.W. Woolworth store in Frankfort, Indiana. The long, lonely wait was over. My father, a minister, performed the wedding ceremony, and our 53-year marriage has been a joyful journey.

—*Hillary Howell*
Phoenix, Oregon

Tips for Homemakers: Feeding the Family on a Budget

Dorothy B. Marsh

Although many people lost their savings in the stock market crash and many among the working class lost their jobs and homes, not everyone was destitute during the Depression years. Still, most were forced to alter their lifestyles and live within diminished means. Desperate for work, husbands accepted reduced pay and worked longer hours, leaving their wives to provide for their families on smaller budgets. The following article, written by columnist Dorothy B. Marsh and appearing in the women's magazine *Good Housekeeping* in 1935, advises homemakers on how to feed their families nourishing meals on varying budgets.

W ith food costs going up and incomes staying where they are, many families are finding it necessary to curtail in varying degrees their spending for food. So we are being asked many questions as to how to economize on food budgets and still keep fit.

Planning healthful meals that keep within one's food budget is much like building a house. You can build well-constructed houses at varying costs. But in any case, you must know what is required to build soundly the foundation, framework, roof, walls, etc. So, too, in building healthful meals, you must know the needs of your family, and then select foods that will supply these needs for the amount of money which you can afford to spend.

And now comes the inevitable question: "How shall I know which combinations of foods to serve to keep my family fit, and still not run over my food budget?"

Few of us housekeepers have the time either to delve deeply into a study of nutrition or to count calories every time we plan

Dorothy B. Marsh, "Delicious Meals to Fit Your Pocketbook," *Good Housekeeping*, vol. XCX, January 1935, pp. 81–83.

a meal. Fortunately, this is not necessary. For [in this article] you will find two Measuring Sticks for Daily Meals which the [Good Housekeeping] Institute has prepared for you—one for those who are trying to keep to low-cost food budgets, and the other for those who wish to follow moderate or more liberal food budgets.

Choose the Measuring Stick which fits your particular needs and use it for checking up or measuring the healthfulness of your meals for the day. It will tell you whether or not your daily meals are adequate. It will do away with the tedious balancing of every meal by telling you in an instant what foods your meals should provide every day. It will also help you in buying food, for it shows you how to spend your food budget wisely for the foods which are necessary to health.

Take the Measuring Stick for Low-Cost Meals, for example. Because of its short, concise form, you can tell at a glance just what low-cost foods you can and should serve daily to each member of your family to keep him healthy and happy. It does not talk about proteins, carbohydrates, minerals, vitamins, etc., but only of groups of foods which supply these things at low cost. And when food from each of the groups in the Measuring Stick is eaten in sufficient amount every day, one is assured of an adequate supply of energy-giving foods, body-building proteins, and the all-important minerals and vitamins.

Foods that go into the making of low-cost meals are necessarily more limited in variety than those in the moderate and more liberal food budgets, as our Measuring Stick shows. And the smaller the food budget, the less variety it is possible to have. Milk is the foundation of low-cost meals, and important it is, too, that each member of the family have his full quota. But the amounts of meat and eggs must be pared down, and the less expensive meat cuts used. Limited, too, is the variety of fruits and vegetables, for they must be of the low-cost kind. Also bread and other cereals must appear much more frequently and in more liberal amounts in low-cost meals, for they furnish fuel for the body more cheaply than any other food.

While considering food values, however, do not forget for one moment that whether your meals are low, moderate, or liberal in cost, they should be made not only healthful but interesting; that all the foods should be made as delicious as possible; and that they should be served attractively, too.

To show you just how to use our Measuring Sticks in planning healthful as well as interesting daily meals—whatever your food budget—the Institute planned meals for four days. . . .

The day's menus for the limited and low-cost meals were planned with the Measuring Stick for Low-Cost Meals . . . as a pattern. The menus for the moderate and liberal meals were planned with the Measuring Stick for Moderate-Cost Meals . . . as a pattern. And while we did not attempt to quote prices—because of the differences in food prices throughout the country, and seasonal fluctuations in prices—you can readily see from our menus that, as the variety of expensive fruits, vegetables, meats, etc., is increased in the day's meals, the cost level of those meals increases, too. Therefore—and it's a lucky break—if, in planning your own family meals, you find that a certain day's meals cost a bit more than your budget permits, due perhaps to the serving of some favorite dish particularly enjoyed by the family, you can balance costs by serving less expensive but none the less nourishing foods the next day.

A Measuring Stick for Low-Cost Meals

What to Serve Each Day for Grown-Ups and Children Over Five Years

1. One qt. milk for each child, either as a beverage, on cereals, or as an ingredient of soups, sauces, desserts, etc. One pt. milk for each adult.
2. Some fruit or tomatoes, three or four times a week and oftener if possible.
3. Potatoes once a day.
4. At least one vegetable other than potatoes, such as carrots, onions, yellow turnips, beets, peas, parsnips, dried beans, or lentils each day. A leafy vegetable, such as string beans, cabbage, spinach, etc., three or four times a week.
5. A raw vegetable, such as chopped cabbage or spinach or grated carrots three or four times a week. Plan to serve such a vegetable on the days when the budget does not permit fruit or tomatoes. Cut vegetable into strips for children over 4 years of age; this encourages jaw exercise and is good for tooth development.

6. Bread or cereals (including flour, spaghetti, and rice), one or both at each meal.
7. An egg three or four times a week, especially for children.
8. Fats in moderate amounts.
9. Simple desserts in moderate amounts to carry milk, cereals, etc., and to supply energy.
10. As your food budget permits, add cheese, meat, or fish dishes daily.
11. Crisp bread, such as toast, bread sticks, hard crackers, with every meal for children, to give necessary jaw exercise and to provide for tooth development.
12. Cod-liver oil is beneficial to all. Especially needed by children up to eight years of age, particularly during the winter months. Allow two teaspoonfuls daily.
13. Plenty of drinking water, fresh air, and sleep.

A Measuring Stick for Moderate-Cost Meals

What to Serve Each Day for Grown-Ups and Children Over Five Years

1. One qt. milk for each child, either as a beverage, on cereals, or as an ingredient of such dishes as soups, sauces, desserts, etc. One pt. milk for each adult.
2. Fruit twice a day if possible. To insure enough vitamin C, select either oranges or tomatoes as one of these fruits. For the other fruit, select a fresh, canned, or cooked dried fruit.
3. Potatoes once a day. Two other vegetables—one a green leafy vegetable, such as string beans, spinach, cabbage, beet and turnip tops, etc.
4. A salad of lettuce, raw cabbage, carrot, etc., once a day. Cut the raw vegetable into strips for children over 4 yrs. of age: this encourages jaw exercise and is good for tooth development.
5. Cereal for breakfast, and bread with each meal, including some of the whole-grain varieties.
6. An egg once a day for each child, and if possible for each adult.
7. A meat, fish, or cheese dish once a day.
8. Macaroni, rice, dried peas, beans, lentils, for lunch or sup-

per dishes, or occasionally as a substitute for meat.
9. Butter each day, and moderate amounts of salad oil and other fats.
10. Simple desserts in moderate amounts to carry milk, cereals, etc., and to supply energy.
11. Cod-liver oil is beneficial to all. Especially needed by children up to eight years of age, particularly during the winter months. Allow two teaspoonfuls daily.
12. Crisp bread, such as toast, bread sticks, hard crackers, with every meal for children, to give necessary jaw exercise and to provide for tooth development.
13. Plenty of drinking water, fresh air, and sleep.

Food Budgets

If you are using one of our Measuring Sticks as a guide in planning daily meals for a family with children, we believe that you will also find the following tables prepared by Dr. Hazel K. Stiebeling, of the United States Bureau of Home Economics, helpful in dividing up what you have to spend on food. These tables suggest a proper division of the money in very limited, low-cost, moderate, and liberal food budgets, to insure healthful meals. . . .

Planning Meals On a Very Limited Food Budget
Allow 25% to 30% of your money for milk and cheese
Allow 25% to 20% of your money for fruits and vegetables
Allow 10% of your money for lean meat, fish, and eggs
Allow 20% of your money for bread, flour, and cereals
Allow 20% of your money for fats, sugars, and accessories

Planning Meals On a Low-Cost Food Budget
Allow 30% to 35% of your money for milk and cheese
Allow 25% to 20% of your money for fruits and vegetables
Allow 15% of your money for lean meat, fish, and eggs
Allow 15% of your money for bread, flour, and cereals
Allow 15% of your money for fats, sugars, and accessories

Planning Meals On a Moderate Food Budget
Allow 25% to 30% of your money for milk and cheese
Allow 30% to 25% of your money for fruits and vegetables

Allow 20% to 15% of your money for lean meat, fish, and eggs
Allow 10% of your money for bread, flour, and cereals
Allow 15% to 20% of your money for fats, sugar, and accessories

Planning Meals On a Liberal Food Budget
Allow 30% of your money for milk, cheese, butter, and cream
Allow 30% of your money for fruits and vegetables
Allow 25% to 30% of your money for lean meat, fish, and eggs
Allow 15% to 10% of your money for bread, flour, cereals, fats, sugars, and accessories
Note: Families of adults will spend relatively less for milk, perhaps more for fats, sugars, and cereals, and more for lean meat, fish, and eggs than families with children.
And now for a few recipes. . . .

A Day's Meals for a Very Limited Food Budget

BREAKFAST
Hot Cooked Cereal   Milk
Toast   Margarine
Coffee (adults)   Milk (children)

LUNCHEON
Scalloped Macaroni and Tomatoes
Cabbage Salad
Bread   Margarine
(Toast for Children)
Cocoa for all

DINNER
Lamb Stew with Potatoes, Onions, and Carrots
Bread   Margarine
(Toast for Children)
Indian Pudding
Milk (children)

Note: Use evaporated milk diluted with an equal amount of water for cooking. Use undiluted evaporated milk for coffee.

Use bottled pasteurized milk for cereal and drinking. Add tomato juice to breakfast of young children. In buying bread include some of whole-wheat variety. Allow 2 tsp. cod-liver oil daily for each child up to 8 yrs., especially during the winter months. . . .

A Day's Meals for a Low-Cost Food Budget

BREAKFAST
Sliced Oranges
Hot Cooked Cereal   Milk
Toast   Butter
Coffee (adults)   Cocoa (children)

LUNCHEON
Scalloped Cheese and Hominy
Cabbage and Apple Salad
Bread   Butter
(Toast for children)
Norwegian Prune Pudding
Milk (children)

DINNER
Hamburger Chowder with Tomatoes and Potatoes
Bread   Butter
(Toast for children)
Creamy Rice Pudding
Milk (children)

Note: Use evaporated milk diluted with an equal amount of water for cooking. Use bottle pasteurized milk for cereal and drinking. In buying the bread include some of the whole-wheat variety. Use hot milk or top milk in the coffee. Allow 2 tsp. cod-liver oil daily for each child up to 8 yrs., especially during the winter months. . . .

A Day's Meals for a Moderate Food Budget

BREAKFAST
Sliced Bananas
Ready-to-Serve or Hot Cooked Cereal   Milk

Soft Cooked Eggs
Toast   Butter
Coffee (adults)   Cocoa (children)

LUNCHEON
Cheese and Spaghetti Casserole   Green Pea Sauce
Toast   Butter
Raisin and Carrot Salad   Cooked Salad Dressing
Tea (adults)   Milk (children)

DINNER
Scallopine of Veal with Tomatoes and Onions
Boiled Potatoes   Mashed Turnips
Bread   Butter
(Toast for children)
Butterscotch Pudding   Top Milk
Coffee (adults)   Milk (children)

Note: Use bottled pasteurized milk for cereal and drinking. Use evaporated milk diluted with an equal amount of water for cooking. Use light cream for coffee. In buying the bread include some of whole-wheat variety. Allow 2 tsp. cod-liver oil daily for each child up to 8 yrs., especially during the winter months. . . .

A Day's Meals for a Liberal Food Budget
BREAKFAST
Orange Juice
Ready-to-Serve or Hot Cooked Cereal   Milk
Scrambled Eggs
Toast   Butter
Coffee (adults)   Cocoa (children)

LUNCHEON
Kidney Bean Soup   Crackers
Cabbage and Beet Salad
Bread   Butter
Baked Caramel Custard
Milk (children)

DINNER
Cod Steaks Baked in Cheese Sauce
Mashed Potatoes   Casserole of Spinach and Tomatoes
Celery
Bread   Butter
(Toast for children)
Chocolate Meringue Pie
Coffee (adults)

Note: Use bottled pasteurized milk for drinking, cereal, Cheese Sauce, and Mashed Potatoes. Use evaporated milk diluted with an equal amount of water for the cocoa, Baked Caramel Custard, salad dressing, and Chocolate Pie. Use light cream for the coffee. In buying the bread include some of the whole-wheat variety. Allow 2 tsp. cod-liver oil daily for each child up to 8 yrs., especially during the winter months.

The Struggle to Stay in School

Robert Cohen

The Great Depression was hard for young people; it interrupted their childhoods by putting more hardship and responsibility on their shoulders than children usually have to handle. In particular, it was difficult for children to stay in school. Some children quit school to look for work; others dropped out because their families moved so much looking for work. Lack of money, transportation, and clothing, however, were the major challenges for many children. Seeking help, thousands of children living through the Depression wrote to the First Lady, Eleanor Roosevelt, for all kinds of assistance. Roosevelt received requests for money, clothing, bicycles, advice—all with the hope that she, with her reputation for kindness and generosity, would be able to answer their call. Unfortunately, Roosevelt was rarely able to help these children—her assistants answered many letters, but many others were probably never opened. Robert Cohen edited a collection of some of these letters in his book *Dear Mrs. Roosevelt: Letters from Children of the Great Depression.* Cohen is director of the social studies program in the Steinhardt School of Education, an associate professor in the department of teaching and learning, and an affiliated member of the history department at New York University. The following excerpt includes letters to the First Lady from children seeking her help in staying in school.

Teachers, administrators, and government officials wrote and said much about the shortcomings of American education during the Great Depression. They told of school closings, shortened academic terms, cuts in teacher salaries, and harsh retrenchment in many school budgets, especially during the early 1930s. Few school systems were unaffected by hard times. But as the report of President [Franklin] Roosevelt's Advisory Committee on Education revealed in 1938, the Depression's burdens were not equally distributed. Rural, southern, and black schools entered the Depression as the nation's most poorly funded, and they could least afford the declines in school budgets wrought by the economic crisis. The National Education Association estimated that by 1934 rural poverty had closed more than 20,000 schools. In 1935–36, white students attending school in Arkansas, Mississippi, Alabama, Georgia, and South Carolina received less than half the national average of per pupil spending (which then stood at $74.30), and less than a third of the spending on students in such better-funded states as New York. Black students in Georgia, Mississippi, and South Carolina received less than a tenth of the national average of per pupil spending.

That these were hard times for schools, families, and the young becomes even clearer when one looks at the birth rate and grade school enrollments. The Depression decade was not one into which adults were eager to bring children, and the birth rate fell accordingly. Declining birth rates shrank primary school populations. Between 1930 and 1938 the number of five-year-old children in the United States declined by 17.3 percent, yielding a 16.1 percent decline in kindergarten enrollments. The number of students enrolled in the first four school grades dropped annually between 1930 and 1934, in the first seven grades between 1934 and 1938.

The educational picture was not entirely gloomy, however. Because of the tremendous shortage of jobs for the young, the Depression kept students in school longer than their pre-Depression predecessors—in the 1930s they had nowhere else to go. This trend was accelerated by the student aid program of the National Youth Administration. High school enrollments rose from 4,399,422 at the opening of the Depression decade to 6,545,991 at the end of the decade. These same factors led (after a brief dip from 1932 to 1934) to a rise in college enrollments during the second half of the Depression decade: in 1939 the college population was 1.3 million, surpassing the pre-Depression peak of 1.1 million.

These rather contradictory educational trends in Depression America must be kept in mind when one reads the letters that students of all grade levels sent to Mrs. Roosevelt. The letters reflect both trends: the economic stress and inadequate school resources of the 1930s, as school systems lacked the funds to transport their students to and from school, and could not provide them with free textbooks or even secondhand clothes; and, at the same time, the new expectations created by the surging school population in the upper grades. With the rise in school retention rates and an increasing number of students staying in school longer, youths came to feel that continued academic enrollment, at least through high school, was the norm, and that it would be unfair for their own poverty to keep them from enjoying the educational opportunities available to so many other young Americans. Thus the students' letters reflect both the limited educational resources and the expansive educational aspirations of Depression youth. . . .

The . . . letters [to Mrs. Roosevelt that focus] on education . . . contain a variety of requests, all stemming from their desire to stay in school. Clothing was the most common item that children and teens asked Mrs. Roosevelt to help them secure. The majority of requests came of dire necessity: as a relief worker from Arkansas observed in 1935, "I find so many children do not get to go to school because they simply haven't a rag that they can leave home in."

Along with deficiencies caused by family poverty, the letters reflect shortcomings caused by the limitations of the educational system itself. The 1930s were a time when location, especially in poor rural areas, placed grave limitations on access to secondary schooling. Students who lived on isolated farms or in small towns often had to struggle to find ways to commute or move to the nearest large town—what one of the letter writers termed "a high school town"—so that they could continue their education. This caused hardships when the towns were a long way off or had rents that proved too dear for low-income students, so students of high school age often asked Eleanor Roosevelt for help with these expenses. . . .

After graduation from secondary school only about 10 percent of college-age Americans were able to go on to college during the Depression. America's college population included a sizable minority, thousands of students, who pursued their dreams of higher education even though economically they could not really afford to do so. . . .

The Depression had decimated the stock market, devastated industrial production, and staggered the rural economy, but it could not still the longings of the young to improve themselves through formal education. . . .

Requests for Money

Amarillo, Texas

Jan. 4, 1934

Dear Mrs. Roosevelt,

I am a young girl eighteen years of age and in the ninth grade. I have always had a hope of completing high school any way. When I was bearly fourteen I graduated from the 8th grade at Halister, Oklahoma. My folks then moved to New Mexico and have made four crop failures and have been unable to send me to school last year for 2½ months. I worked my way thro school, and by hard work studing and prayer I made four whole high school credits. . . . This year I wanted to go so bad I left home and came to Amarillo thinking I could find a place to work for my room and board. I succeeded up until Christmas but since more students came in I can't find a place any where and really don't know what I shall do. It takes $150 to go thro school. This pays for my tuition, cloths, board and books. I have sold candy for part of my books but only make 75 cents a week to my part this did not meet the full demand. In 3 years I can finish if I can go on which I hope to do. I just wander if you could help me some. It will only take $140 a year & I can finish in 3 years with this year.

I have always wanted to get an education but for so long (nearly four years) I had lost almost all hopes. A number of the people makes fun of me being so old & in such a low grade but I am willing to stand all the cuffs and huffs to get through school. I go to the S.O. 7 School in Amarillo. I hope to hear from you soon as I'm in great need. I have a place to stay until the 15th of Jan. then if I can't get some money somewhere to help me I can never make this term. Any thing you can do will be oh so much appreciated. For I see my need to schooling and I so long to get an education. I have been making from 90–100 on most everything.

Your unseen friend,

E.S.

East Point, Ky.

Jan. 31, 1934

Dear Mrs. Roosevelt,

I am a girl sixteen years old. In 1930 I was a freshman in the Painteville High School but had to quit going on account of the depression. Since then financial difficulties have kept me from going to school anywhere, even a public school. The Painteville High school was the nearest school to my home. And it was about seven miles away. When I was going I had to get out of bed at 5:30 ever morning at 6:45 I had to leave home. I live on the river so I had to cross it in a boat. Sometime when it would be raining or snowing I would have to change shoes when I got across. And in winter when I started from home it would be so dark I could hardly see. Then I had to walk one mile on the railroad before I could get to the bus line. My parents worked hard to keep me in school. I wanted a good education and a chance in the world. And they wanted me to have it but since we live on a farm and could sell nothing it wasn't long until I had to quit school. My father had many debts he had to pay so of course he could not pay them and send me to school even though I was going to a public school he found it hard to buy my clothes, books, pay for my bus fare, etc. so there was nothing left for me to do but quit. Mrs. Roosevelt I am writing the truth today there is only $2.07 in money that we can call our own. Of course, we have some things to sell but noone wants to buy anything.

And now I am going to ask a favor of you although I don't know what you will think of me for doing so. I want you to send me enough money so that I can finish High School. I will not ask you to give me any. I want you to know and believe I will pay it back when ever I can although it might be years before I could. I wouldn't ask you but I though that since it couldn't mean much to you but would mean everything to me may be you might. If you couldn't lend me much a small amount would help me more than I can tell you. I might never be able to pay it back but I hope so.

Please Mrs. Roosevelt let me hear from you.

Yours very truly

M.L.A. . . .

Big Rock, Tennessee
[acknowledged Aug. 3, 1934]
Mrs. Franklin D. Roosevelt

Don't cast this away unread. Its not a sob story though it does sound pretty sobby.

Whether writing you is the thing I should, or should not do, I don't know, but I feel as if you'll not be offended because you were a school teacher once—Were you not?

My trouble is this—I am eighteen years of age and ready to enter school as a sophomore this term which begins Sept. 3. But the main thing is I *cant* attend. With me life has always been just a day to day existence, but I've managed (or Dad has) to be in school this far. As a studious girl I've always made good. My grades in my final exams last term were 97-98-99-100. My friends and teachers encourage me to finish school, and, oh, I do want to—but it seems impossible, and is impossible with us. I

Eleanor Roosevelt happily poses with a group of schoolchildren. Thousands of poor children requested her help to stay in school.

thought perhaps you'd understand and would help me, well I'm ashamed to ask it but if I have to fall out of school it means the last of my hopes, for my one ambition is to be a writer.

I've always wanted to write and have tried both poetry and short stories. I have a collection of these on hand but writers are not made overnight and I know the road to authorship is a hard one. With an education it would be hard for a poor country girl like me but without even a high school education it means "you're just a flop." My English teacher said that I had talent and if I would keep on I could reach success but how can I "keep on keeping on" with no backing?

I hope you understand, I hope you help me, yet do you understand, how could you? You've never been a farm girl like me. Can you imagine getting up before "Sun-up" and going to work in the tobacco patch and all the time be thinking of school days comming when there'll be no school for you, thinking of the hundreds of old memories and things that happen in school life, thinking of the old pals you've been separated from so long, thinking of the gossips that will wag their tongues when you drop from the school gang and thinking last, *What will I ever amount to?* No, you can't imagine it, who could unless they've had experience as I have?

Can you imagine how hard it is to be eighteen—just in the morning of womanhood when life should be at its highest, to have all your plans and hopes crushed, To have to refuse all the gaiety and pleasure that a young girl should have just because your clothing is not sufficient? Well that's how it is with me. Last week a friend asked me why I had quit coming to church—it embarrassed me but I told the truth. My shoes were not fit to be seen in public!

Dad can't buy for me. He can't get the necessary things for home life—Why? He and I have all that we can do to keep our crop worked, Mother's pregnant, and Dad would have to desert his crop if he *could* find work.

I hope you don't think me a crank for I really am not. It hurts me to ask but could you—would you, help me personally, to attend school? Surely a woman like you can understand.

Respectfully,

R.C.T.

Requests for Clothing

Humboldt, Kansas
　　Jan. 5, 1935
　　My Dear Mrs. Roosevelt:
　　Would you have time to read a letter from just a country girl? I will be sixteen years old March 22. I am a senior in High School.

　　We worked hard during the campaign for Mr. Roosevelt, our Democratic club (young peoples) had meetings and gave short programs before the speaking. I was on the programs all over the county for tap dances.

　　Here is my problem. We raised no grain and money is scarce. My father was seriously injured two months ago, which made it still harder. I need clothes for school but haven't funds to buy them. I just wondered if you might have some I could make over, as I do all my own sewing—which is mostly madeover. I would appreciate anything as I have to go ten miles to school and I have no overshoes or not very good shoes.

　　Dresses, hose that can be mended and used, shoes, overshoes or underwear. I wear 6½ shoes and a 16 dress.

　　If you can help me—write me.
　　Thank you.
　　Sincerely
　　P.S. Please do not let this be put in the newspapers.

　　Drumright, Okla.
　　January 16, 1935
　　Mrs. Roosevelt:
　　I am a girl, age fourteen (14), and in the eleventh grade, I am five feet, three inches tall, have brown hair and blue eyes, and weigh about 130 pounds. I have gone to school eight years, all of which my mother has paid for. My parents were divorced before I started to school, and my father, who is married again and has children, does not help us any. I have 1 brother, aged sixteen (16) who is also in the eleventh grade. He is taller than I am but weighs several pounds less. We are both at the head of our class, and have been exempted from all our semester "exams" so far.

　　We desire to go to college when we finish high school, and if we can manage the clothes and money, maybe have to work our way through, we will, if at all possible. My brother wishes to be a lawyer and enter politics, and I want to be a primary school teacher, an author, and a church and Welfare worker. I teach a class of girls, age 4 to 8 each Sunday and my brother, a class of boys, 4 to 9.

We lived in town for a while and Mother worked, but we had to come to the country over four years ago. My brother and I pick cotton each year for our clothes and Mother keeps house for a man, who surely does like, Mr. Roosevelt's new Deal. Since there was so little cotton this year we didn't have very much money to buy the clothes that we *have* to have.

We go to a high school six miles from home, and walk two miles waiting in the cold till the truck comes. We have no car, no radio, or any other musical instrument.

I am writing this letter to ask if you have any cast-off clothing or any wearing apparel you don't want. I would certainly appreciate them and Mother could make them over to fit me. If you have anything which isn't already spoken for, it would be new to me and I could surely use it. It costs a "lot of money" to keep in dresses, hats, slippers, hose, coats, underthings and everything else that a person needs and I don't have that "lot of money" to spare because it takes so much to go to school.

I would always remember you for the kindness you would be sharing, if you would send me some of your things that you have no longer any use for. I don't want you to think I am begging you for anything, but I'm merely asking for some cast-offs you don't want. I could use *anything* and it would surely make my Senior year in high school, much easier.

Your friend,

S.A.

P.S.—I'll tell all our friends what fine people you Roosevelts are in the next Presidential Election. . . .

Harrodsburg, Ky.

December 18, 1933

Dear Mrs. Roosevelt,

I wrote you more than a week ago but, never recieve any responds from you. Please help me, if you think that much I ask you were to much Why not Loan me the amount of $18.75 for

Debt on Sewing ring, Pin and invitation cards and if you have any old white dress, an old crep dress I can rite for my class dress an old dress for the senior, and junior prom, an old grey cap and sward you know what I am trying to explain to you. Your husband, son, daughter, and your self have been through the same thing of what I am going through, I mean graduation but, still not like me, you all of high class could finance yours and look forward to a happy graduation why I am of poor class no parents, no means by which to finance my graduation in any way. It is a pleasure to graduate but, it gives me more heart aches than pleasure. At night it is a constance worry with me wondering just what to do, or how to do, to go about doing some thing. I haven't any job and can't get one, holding the class back, who have their money for their things and waiting on me to bring mine. Please shut your eyes for a while just imaging you are in my predictment. Please understand and help me. If you would send the clothes to I can make them over during the holidays and pay for my things just as soon as I can give the secretary of my class the money to send to Lexington, Ky.

Mr. E. our superintendent of Harrodsburg, Ky, Mr. J.R. of Frankfort Ky our superintendent and Mrs. S. have been very good to give me my books and a few clothes Please help me and please don't disappoint me as I know no one else to help me, write in care of Mrs. M.E.C. old lady I stay with for food and room

A very anxious poor girl

H.L.M.

P.S.

Hopen to hear from you at once (Please)

The Works Progress Administration Handbook

Works Progress Administration

The Works Progress Administration (WPA) was an initiative of the Franklin Roosevelt administration to tackle unemployment and get Americans back on their feet. The program, directed by Harry Hopkins, began with the aim of creating jobs for skilled workers including scientists, doctors, seamstresses, teachers, welders, foresters, musicians, actors, and painters. The program also provided jobs to unskilled laborers. According to some statistics, the WPA employed 8.5 million people on more than a million projects between its inception in 1935 and its demise in 1943. The following excerpt is taken from the handbook produced by the WPA to answer questions for current and prospective employees.

*Q*uestion. What is WPA?
Answer. The WPA is one of several Federal agencies established by the President and Congress to bring about recovery by giving work to the unemployed.

Q. Are there other agencies of the Government that have been set up to provide work for the unemployed?

A. Yes. Among these are the Public Works Administration (PWA), Civilian Conservation Corps (CCC), Resettlement Administration (RA).

Q. What is the largest number of workers these agencies ever employed?

A. During February 1936 the total number of men and women working was 3,853,000. As a result of an increase in private industry and seasonal agricultural employment more than 500,000 fewer are employed on work projects now (July 1936).

Q. Does the WPA give relief without work?

Works Progress Administration, *WPA Worker's Handbook*, 1936.

A. No. Direct relief is generally taken care of by the local people.

Q. Can any unemployed person get a job on WPA?

A. No, only those able-bodied unemployed persons who are in greatest need and who have been so certified by a local agency.

Q. Will all those certified by such local agency be given work?

A. Not necessarily. WPA is limited by the amount of money appropriated by Congress.

Q. How many people in one family are allowed to work on WPA?

A. Generally only one. If the family has a boy in the CCC camps or one of the family is getting work with the National Youth Administration (NYA), that does not necessarily keep the head of the family from working on WPA. Of course, no one under 18 years of age can be hired, except in NYA.

Q. Can old people or sick people work on WPA?

A. Certainly not if they are sick or so old that it is not safe for them or for others who work around them.

Q. Do race or color or beliefs keep a man from getting work on WPA?

A. No.

Women

Q. Do these rules apply to women workers as well as men?

A. Yes. (There are about 400,000 women working in the WPA.)

What Are WPA Jobs?

Q. Why does the WPA have these projects?

A. In order to provide employment on useful projects for you and for other qualified persons who cannot find employment in private industry.

Q. Is WPA the same thing as emergency relief?

A. No. When we had the Emergency Relief Program, many workers did not get a chance to work for the money they received. Under WPA you earn a monthly wage for the work you do.

Q. When I take a Government job, am I still on relief?

A. No. You are off relief. You are working.

Q. What is the chance of getting a job at my regular trade?

A. If you are not working at your regular trade on the project, it is probably because there are no jobs open for your particular trade. This is one of the toughest problems the Work Program has had to meet, because the Government projects don't call for many different trades. Many skilled workers have to take common labor jobs. For example, it is impossible to hire skilled miners, skilled tailors, and skilled weavers on Government projects. The Work Program does not have projects like these, because they would interfere with private business. You should file an application at the National Reemployment Service office for work at the trade you know. They will let you know if they get a call for a man of your experience.

How Long Will the Jobs Last?

Q. How long will WPA jobs last?

A. The Government is making every effort to diminish the Work Program as rapidly as private jobs can be found by the workers who are in need because of the depression. Congress made a second appropriation of money for WPA to continue the work.

Q. Do I lose my job when the project I am working on is finished?

A. Not necessarily. You should be reassigned to another job. There may be a delay. It is not easy to keep millions of people constantly at work, and workers themselves will have to help keep things going.

Questions Workers Most Often Ask

Q. At what rate will I be paid?

A. You will receive a monthly wage which will be figured at the hourly rate of pay prevailing in your locality for the occupation. The number of hours of work per month is established by dividing your local hourly rate into your monthly wage.

Q. How often will I be paid?

A. Most projects pay twice a month.

Q. Do I get my pay promptly at the end of a work period?

A. No. There is generally several days' delay in getting your check. This is because the timekeeper has to make out the pay roll to show who has worked. Then the pay roll has to be sent to the office so the checks can be made out. If you have to wait more than a few days, ask your foreman or project supervisor about it.

Q. Do all workers get the same monthly wage?

A. No. In general, the more skill the job requires, the more the pay will be.

Q. What are some other reasons for differences in pay?

A. Workers who live in big cities generally get more than those who live in small towns and in the country because it costs more to live in big cities.

Q. Are mistakes sometimes made in setting wages in different cities and for different jobs?

A. Yes. Mistakes are sure to be made in giving work to millions of unemployed people. Some mistakes have already been corrected. Others will be corrected as they are found.

Q. Is it possible to have the monthly wage or the hourly rate increased?

A. This is possible only if facts justify a change. WPA officials have to be governed by the rules as set up under the law, and by conditions prevailing in the locality. If you have questions you should submit them to the local or State WPA offices.

Q. Where will I be paid?

A. Your checks will be mailed to you or delivered to you on the job.

Q. How can I get a raise in pay?

A. Work on these projects is paid for according to four classifications of work: Unskilled, intermediate (semiskilled), skilled, professional and technical. If there is a higher paid job available for which you are trained, you can apply for a reclassification. If you are reclassified from unskilled to intermediate or skilled, you will get the higher pay. Much depends on local customs.

Things You Can Be Docked For

Q. Do I get docked for being late or absent?

A. Yes. The foreman will tell you how much you lose for being late or absent.

Q. What if I get sick—does my pay go on?

A. No.

Q. What if I stay away from the job because I went to do something else?

A. You will not be paid for any time you do not work.

Q. Can my wages be pledged, assigned, or garnished?

A. No.

Q. How much money can be taken out of my monthly earnings if I am put up in a work camp?

A. If your project is so far away from town that it takes too much time to go to and from work every day and a camp is set up at the project, some of your pay will be deducted for your food and shelter. The amount deducted will be determined by your State Administrator.

Q. When a job is completed or postponed, does my pay go on?

A. No.

Q. Do I get paid while I am waiting to be assigned to another job?

A. No.

Q. Is there any way I can make up lost time?

A. You are paid only for the time you actually work, but you will be allowed every reasonable opportunity to make up time lost because of weather conditions or temporary interruptions beyond your control. Such lost time may be made up in the current or succeeding pay-roll months, as the job permits.

Working Time

Q. Do all workers have to put in the same number of hours on WPA projects?

A. No, but no worker may be required to work more than 8 hours per day, 40 hours per week, or 140 hours in two semi-monthly pay periods, except to make up lost time or in extreme emergencies. This rule is only for WPA and not for other governmental agencies.

Q. Who can change the number of hours I have to work?

A. The WPA Administrator of your State can change the number of hours per day, week, or month; but the hours cannot be more than 8 per day, 40 per week, or 140 in two semimonthly pay periods, except to make up lost time or in extreme emergencies.

Q. If there is an emergency and I have to work more than the usual number of hours, can I be paid for overtime?

A. No. If you are required to work overtime, your hours will be shorter on another day to make up for the extra time you worked. It is against the law to pay any Government employee in the country for overtime.

Q. If it rains or the project is held up for some other reason such as not having materials, do I get a cut in salary?

A. Yes, unless you can make up the lost time.

Q. Will I get paid for holidays if I don't work?

A. No. You get paid only when you work.

Dismissals

Q. Can I be fired from the job?

A. Yes. You can be fired if your work is not satisfactory.

Q. If I am fired from a project, does that mean that I can't get another Government job?

A. No. If your conduct justifies it, you may get another chance. Ask to be reinstated.

Q. Suppose I am fired for reasons I think are unfair. What can I do?

A. If you think your discharge was unfair, you can appeal to the local WPA officials. If they rule against you, you can appeal to the State officials, and if you are still ruled against and you are not satisfied you may appeal to the Labor Policies Board at the general offices of the Works Progress Administration, Washington, D.C. NOTE.—Foremen, supervisors, and other WPA officials have many troublesome problems in trying to keep the projects going, and to keep you supplied with tools and a job. They have a right to expect your cooperation in their efforts to see that an orderly and efficient job is done.

Complaints

Q. Do I have a right to complain about wages, hours, and other things?

A. Yes. You can complain to the foreman, the local WPA office, the State Administrator, or the Labor Policies Board in Washington.

Q. May a union of project workers send a representative or delegate to the WPA district officials to adjust grievances?

A. Yes.

Q. Does the representative have to be a WPA worker?

A. No.

Q. Does the Government give extra help to workers who have been sick and lost pay?

A. No. If you need extra help, you will have to get it from the city or county officials or some private agency.

Q. If I am ill, will I get free medical attention from the WPA?

A. No.

Accidents and Compensation

Q. Do I get compensation if I am hurt on the job? If so, what do I get?

A. Yes. The most you can get is $25 per month. NOTE.—All

safety rules should be carefully followed.

Q. When does my compensation begin if I am hurt?

A. It begins 3 days after your injury is reported.

Q. Where can I find out more about compensation?

A. Every work project has a large cardboard sign with the compensation rules on it. You should read and study it. One of these rules says: "Secure first-aid treatment. Do not neglect small injuries. Blood poisoning or permanent disability or death might result." This is very important.

Safety

Q. Is equipment provided to protect us from injury?

A. Yes. Either the Government or the sponsor of the project will provide goggles, safety belts, or life-lines, to protect you against eye injury, dust, falling when working in quarries, tree-trimming jobs, and other dangers.

Q. Am I expected to work in dangerous places if I am afraid of falling?

A. No. If you get dizzy on scaffolds or around trenches, you should tell your foreman. He doesn't want you to get hurt and will put you at other work.

Q. Am I supposed to work in water without boots on?

A. No. You should have boots. You should provide your own if you possibly can. If you cannot, the sponsor or the Government will furnish boots if the work requires it.

Q. Is it part of my job to look after my own safety?

A. Yes. You should be careful at all times so you will not get hurt or hurt other workers.

Q. Should I report unsafe conditions?

A. Yes. Tell your foreman if you notice any conditions that may cause an accident, or if trucks are speeding or drivers are careless around workmen, or if trenches or scaffolds are not safely braced, or lumber or other things are not properly piled.

Q. Should I report defective tools?

A. Yes, especially cracked wedges or mushroomed drillheads, dull axes, and splintered handles.

Q. Am I supposed to furnish my own drinking cup?

A. You should, because, if everybody uses the same cup, a disease that someone has might be caught by everybody.

Q. Must I report all injuries?

A. Yes, even minor cuts and scratches. Your first-aid man or your foreman will give you aid until you can get to the doctor, if you need one.

Q. If I disobey safety instructions and am hurt, will I be taken care of?

A. You will be treated for your injury, but if you disobey instructions on purpose you may not get compensation.

Unions

Q. Is it all right for me to join a workers' union?

A. Yes.

Private Jobs

Q. Suppose I get a chance to work at something besides a Government job. Should I take it?

A. Yes, unless you can show good reasons for not taking it.

Q. What are good reasons for not taking a private job?

A. If the job pays substandard wages or has bad working conditions, you do not have to take it.

Q. What if it is to be only a short job?

A. If it is to be a short job, tell your foreman. He should hold your place open for you.

Q. What if the foreman can't keep my job open; can I get back on WPA when the private job ends?

A. If the foreman cannot keep your job open it may be for reasons over which he has no control. You should also ask advice of the WPA Employment Division officials.

Q. Where do I go to apply for work in private business?

A. Go to the National Reemployment Service. Besides supplying workers to Government jobs, the National Reemployment Service gets calls for workers from private businesses and notifies men and women who are registered with them to apply for jobs that are open. Tell the National Reemployment Service what you can do so that they will call you when a private job you can fill comes along, and keep in touch with them.

Q. If I can get private jobs on holidays and after working hours, will it endanger my WPA job?

A. Not necessarily. This will depend on how much you earn on the side and whether the pay you accept interferes with opportunities of other workers.

General

Q. Does the Government give supplementary relief for large families?

A. No supplementary relief is given by the WPA. Workers who need it should apply to local county or State agencies.

Q. Can I give my work card to some other member of my family if I cannot report for work?

A. No. A work card may only be used by the person whose name is on it.

Getting a Job Near Home

Q. How can I get a job close to my home?

A. The Government tries to place workers as close to their homes as possible, but it is a hard job. Remind the assignment officer until he can make the best possible placement for you.

Carfare

Q. Do I have to pay my own carfare?

A. Sometimes you do and sometimes you don't. You should not have to pay more than the carfare you would pay on any private job.

Your Opinion of the Job You Do

Q. Does the Federal Government select the projects on which we work?

A. No. Practically a hundred percent of the work projects are selected, planned, and supervised by the local community where they are being done. The school board plans the school projects and asks for them. The mayor and city council ask for street projects. The health department asks for sanitary projects. Similar local public agencies ask for others. It is the responsibility of the local government to select good projects and to insist that they be well done.

Q. What if I think the project I am working on is a waste of money; can I complain about it?

A. Yes. All projects are selected by local officials and as a local citizen you should be interested not only in the efficiency but the use the project will be to your community.

Q. If I think the work is valuable, do I have a right to "tell the world"?

A. Yes. If your union or your group wants to hold a celebration when the project is finished, ask your supervisor if he will arrange it, and invite other citizens to come and see it. If it is a school, the school board should help. If it is a park, the park commissioner should help. If it is a road or sewer or waterworks system, the officials of these systems should help. You have added wealth to your community that no depression can take away.

Conclusion

There may be a few things about any big program that we don't like. No matter how hard we try on any big job, something unexpected turns up. The only people who don't make mistakes are those who do nothing at all. The WPA is a great national enterprise to get something done. Mistakes may be made, but we can be sure the American people will not make the mistake of doing nothing.

The Civilian Conservation Corps: "It's a Great Life"

Robert L. Miller

The Civilian Conservation Corps (CCC), the first of President Roosevelt's "New Deal" programs, was instituted in 1933 as a means of fighting America's massive unemployment problem. The CCC promised jobs to all single, physically fit men between the ages of seventeen and twenty-eight. Workers received a dollar a day and were obligated by contract to send all but five dollars of their earnings home to their families every month. The type of work varied, but it was predominantly outdoor physical labor on such projects as constructing bridges, buildings, and dams and developing state parks. Until its end in 1942, the program proved effective against unemployment—approximately 3.5 million men in America were employed by the CCC—but it also accomplished a lot on a more personal level. The slogan of the CCC was "We can take it," which was meant to empower many young men whose confidence was otherwise extremely low during the Depression. Besides a job and three meals a day, the CCC provided a means for learning discipline and self-respect. The program became known as Roosevelt's "peace-time army."

The following essay was written by Robert L. Miller, who worked for the CCC in California. In it, Miller describes how joining the organization helped develop in him a sense of self-respect and pride that was so crucial for young men during the Depression. Miller's spelling, capitalization, and punctuation have been preserved from his original essay.

There is no need to mention much of my life before I enrolled in the Civilian Conservation Corps. It is sufficient to say that the six months previous to my enlistment were most unsatisfactory, from both a financial and mental standpoint. I was often

---

Robert L. Miller, *Success Stories*. National Archives and Records Administration, Record Group 35, Division of Selection, 1937.

hungry, and almost constantly broke.

When I finally enrolled in this great enterprise at Sacramento, California, in October, 1933, I was conscious of Just one thing—I would be fed, clothed, and sheltered during the coming winter. Also I would receive enough actual cash each month to provide the few luxuries I desired.

Feeling of Self-Doubt

The two weeks I had to wait between the time I enrolled and the day we were to leave for camp were given over to much thinking. I began to wonder what kind of a life I was going to live for the next six months. Several questions flashed through my mind. Would I make friends with my fellow members? What kind of work would I be doing? Would I be able to "take it"? This last question was by far the most important to me.

Let me pause for a moment to give you a short character analysis of myself. For years I had been conscious of an inferiority complex that had a firm grip on me. I had tried to hide this complex beneath an outer coating of egotism. To a certain extent I had been successful—I had fooled nearly everyone but myself. Try as I may, I could not overcome the feeling that I was just a little inferior to my fellow men. I did not credit myself with the quality of a leader among men, but how I longed for that virtue. I had always been content to sit back and let someone else get ahead while I wished I were in his boots. It was in this frame of mind that I joined seventy other young men on the morning of October 26, to leave for our camp in the Sierra Nevada Mountains.

Arriving at Camp

Our arrival at camp that same evening was an event that I shall never forget. I was pleasantly surprised at the feeling of genuine hospitality and good cheer that existed among the older members of the company, and reached out to greet we new comers. I had expected a much different atmosphere, and I am ashamed to admit I arrived in camp with a chip on my shoulder. This feeling was soon lost in my pleasant surrounding.

Some of my self-imposed questions were answered in the first two weeks of camp life. Yes, I could make friends with my fellows, and quite easily too. Most of the friendships that I made early in my enlistment have lasted to this day. Some of those friends have left the company, others are with me now. And for those who remain, time has only strengthened the bond between us.

The second question to be answered early in the game was, could I take it? I found that I could and liked it. I could work with these boys, play with them, argue with them and hold up my end. They seemed to like me, and I knew I was fond of them.

This new life had a grip on me, and for the first time in months I was really happy. Good food, plenty of sleep, interesting work and genial companions had created quite a change— my mind was at peace.

Building Confidence

Early in November we moved to our winter camp near Hayward, California. During the period of camp construction that followed our move, I was put in charge of several small jobs. They were insignificant in their nature, but it did me a lot of good Just to think that I was considered reliable enough to boss even a small project. These appointments started me thinking, if I could boss a small job satisfactorily, why couldn't I manage a large one? Then that old feeling would return. I would crawl in my shell and let someone else get the Job I wanted and the raise in pay I coveted.

On December fifteenth several new leaders and assistant leaders were appointed. I held my breath, secretly hoping and praying I would be among the chosen ones. But as usual I was left out, just one of the many, a small cog in a large machine.

One night I went to bed rather early, belay rather tired after a hard days work. Something was wrong, and I didn't fall asleep right away as was my usual custom. I lay awake and thought of many things, finally dwelling on my present situation. My thoughts, when simmered down, were something like this—Here is my big chance to see if I'm going to go ahead in this world, or be Just one of the crowd the rest of my life. I'm Just one man in a group of two hundred young fellows, and I have Just as good a chance as any of the others. So here goes, from now on I'm going to try for advancement—and I'm going to succeed. Such were my thoughts that night, for the first time I realized I had the same chance as the rest to make good.

Next morning in the light of day, things did not look so promising as I had pictured them during the night. But I now had the determination, all I needed was a starting point. In a few days I was to have my start, but it was a queer beginning.

Standing Out from the Crowd

At various times in my life I had done a bit of wrestling, and once or twice had engaged in bouts at camp. I was asked to wrestle a boy in our camp, the bout to be a preliminary to a boxing match between our camp and a neighboring camp, I agreed, not knowing who my opponent was to be. He was not selected until the day of the fight, and when I heard his name I wanted to back out. Pride alone kept me from calling off the bout. My opponent was a huge fellow, weighing twenty-two pounds more than I, and a good three inches taller. No matter how I looked at it, I could picture only a massacre with myself on the losing end. It wasn't fear that made me want to back out, but I dreaded the thought of defeat in front of three or four hundred people.

I climbed into the ring that nite a very doubtful, but determined young man. At least I would put up a good fight. When the bout was over and I emerged the victor, I knew immediately that I had made my start. I was terribly stiff and sore, but very proud and happy. Sleep did not come easily that nite. I was too excited. I kept saying to myself, "I've done it, I'm on my way". Why a physical victory should put me mentally at ease I do not know, but it did.

Then things began to happen rapidly, and soon I became convinced that I was on the right track. A group of sixteen of the most popular boys in camp were forming a club, and I was asked to become a charter member. I was only too glad to Join as most of the boys in the club were either leaders or assistant leaders, and by associating with them I might learn a lot. Election of officers of the club was a prolonged affair but when it was completed, I was the president. For several days I was so excited I had a hard time controlling myself.

At sometime or other, most of us have a friend that has enough interest in our well-being to try to bring us back on the right path after we have gone astray. So it was in my case. There resides in Oakland a young lady whom I have known for several years. As it was only a short distance from camp to Oakland, I was frequently a weekend visitor at her home.

One Sunday afternoon, about a month after my election as president of the club, this young lady and I sat talking in the living room of her home. As we had always been very outspoken with each other, I was not surprised when she said she was going to tell me a few things. I may not have been surprised when she started, but by the time she had finished I'm afraid my face was a trifle red. She told me that in the last month I had changed from a quiet, unassuming young man to a conceited, self-centered prude. She topped it off by saying she could get along very nicely without my company until I recovered from my attack of pig-headedness. That night I slept very little spending most of the nite trying to get things straight in my mind. Out of the chaos of thoughts that came to me I realized two things. First, the young lady was indeed a friend and she had spoken harshly to try to bring me to my senses. Secondly, I realized that my newfound success had gone to my head, and I was making a perfect fool of myself.

For several days I pondered over my problem with no tangible result. It appeared to me that my Job was to strike a happy medium between my old self and this new person that had taken possession of me. I didn't want to go back to the old way, and it was evident that I couldn't continue as I had been doing. The only solution was for me to find an average.

Unconsciously I must have succeeded. Three weeks later when I again visited the young lady for the weekend, she complimented me on my success. She claimed that I was an entirely new person, and she was very very pleased. That Sunday night I returned to camp a very happy young man.

A short time later news came to camp that an Educational Advisor was coming to camp to direct the boys in their pursuit of education. Also we heard that some man in camp was to be appointed to the newly created position of Assistant Educational Advisor. This new position was to carry an assistant leaders rating, which meant a raise in pay for the man lucky enough to get the Job. It wasn't long before a rumor spread through camp that three men were being considered for the new position. Imagine my surprise when I learned from a reliable source that I was one of the three.

On April 6, our Educational Advisor arrived in camp, and that evening I was told I had been appointed his assistant. My goal had been reached. I was at last one of the chosen few. Out of a group of two hundred young men I had been chosen for a position of real importance. Why, I did not know, but I felt sure there must be a reason.

Everything was made clear to me about two weeks later. One evening I was talking to our first lieutenant, he told me how it all came about. It seems the captain was aware of the year and a half I had been to college. He knew I was president of a club that had as its members most of the respected men in camp. He had studied my actions and character when I was not aware I was being watched, and he had decided I was the man for the Job. All this the lieutenant told me, much to my surprise.

In a little less than six months I had literally found myself. For twenty-two years I had doubted my right to call myself a man. My fight had been a long one, and here, in six short months I had proved to myself that I was really a man. A great deal of my success I owe to this certain young lady who brought me back on the right path. But if I had not Joined the Civilian Conservation Corps I never would have made a start.

"Thank God for President Roosevelt and His C.C.C."

I shall try to convey to you Just what the Civilian Conservation Corps has meant to me. There are a great many things of which I could tell, but I shall write of only the most important. The rest I shall keep, deep down in my heart.

First of all, by enrolling in president Roosevelt's peace time army. I managed to retain my self-respect. I did not have to become either a parasite, living off my relatives, or a professional bum. In other words, it gave me a chance to stand on my own two feet and make my own way in the world.

Then it gave me the opportunity to make friendships that will live forever. Nine months of living in close contact with young men of my own age could hardly pass without at least a few lasting friendships. They are fine young men, those chaps who go into the forests of our country to do their bit to preserve our woods, and they are worthy of anyone's friendship. I'm very proud of the friends I've made, and if we should never meet again I can truthfully say they shall never be forgotten.

By living in close contact with these young men I learned the value of appreciating the other fellow's rights. To take one's place among his fellow men and be accepted as a friend is a fine thing for any man.

I had an excellent chance to develop myself physically. Many months of work in the sun have put layers of muscle on my body and turned my skin a dark tan.

But my memories, those golden thoughts that I shall keep forever, are my most valued and treasured keepsake. My album is full of pictures, each one serving as only a starting point for a long Journey into the land of happy days. Days of work in the woods, nights around the fire in the barracks, a trick played on an innocent chap, an all day hike with some of my friends, a fishing trip with one of my pals, the rush for the mess hall when the gong sounds, all of these thoughts are dear to me, and I feel sure that the next few months will bring countless more treasures with each passing day.

These things I have mentioned are benefits derived by every young man who has been a member of the Civilian Conservation Corps. But my personal achievement is the one glorious gift I have received from my association with the young men of the Civilian Conservation Corps.

I enrolled as a boy, unsteady, groping, unsure. I wanted something, but could not describe it or discover a means for attaining it. Then I discovered what it was I was seeking—it was the right to call myself a man. My life at camp has given me that right, and I shall be ever grateful to President Roosevelt and the C.C.C. Now that I am a man, with my feet firmly planted on the steps of life, I feel sure of a reasonable amount of success.

If, in my humble way I have made you realize what the Civilian Conservation Corps has done for me, I am very happy. I do not claim any honor for the change that occurred in me, it just had to be. I'm only deeply thankful that I had the chance to get acquainted with the real me.

So in parting I say "Thank God for President Roosevelt and his C.C.C. I shall never forget you."

A true statement of actual facts by,

Robert L. Miller

Company 999 C.C.C.

Pine Grove, California.

Art and Literature

CHAPTER
2

Chapter Preface

The Works Progress Administration (WPA), one of President Franklin Roosevelt's New Deal initiatives, provided work for thousands of Americans during the Great Depression. Within the WPA were projects geared toward artists and the arts: the Federal Art Project, Federal Writers' Project, Federal Theatre Project, and Federal Music Project provided jobs for the thousands of unemployed actors, singers, musicians, painters, and writers during the Depression years.

Roosevelt felt strongly that art played a significant role in democratic society. His federally funded art programs gave artists an opportunity to work on federally commissioned projects that would contribute to American culture. For example, unemployed writers and journalists were hired to interview former slaves to compile a living history of slavery. State histories were published to provide people with awareness of, and pride in, where they came from. Painters were hired to create murals on the walls of government buildings, and many such murals can still be seen in government buildings throughout the nation. Photographers recorded the Great Depression, leaving heart-rending records that continue to move people today.

Speaking at the Museum of Modern Art in 1939, Roosevelt said that the WPA artist speaks "for the spirit of his fellow countrymen everywhere." Through federally funded art programs, the federal government helped establish that it was not enough to feed people's bellies—one had to feed their souls.

"The Pulps": Fiction for the Masses

Marcus Duffield

Pulp fiction was popular during the Great Depression. "The pulps," as they were known, provided inexpensive fiction that was written quickly and printed on cheap paper. Although not renowned for their literary merit, pulps did provide escape through stories of romance and heroic deeds at a price that was right for people during the 1930s and 1940s. The following is part of a series of articles about publishing in America that appeared in *Vanity Fair* in 1933. In it, contributing writer Marcus Duffield describes the phenomenon of the pulps and the business behind them.

They swarm over the news stands, gaudy, blatant, banal: *Wild West Weekly, Astounding Stories, Ranch Romances*. They are the Pulps, fiction magazines that get their nickname from the fact that their pages are of the very cheapest pulp paper. Into this underworld of literature most of us never dive, unless . . . we are curious about the literary preferences of those who move their lips when they read.

The Pulps are lineal descendants of the old-time dime novels that the current elder generation read under haystacks when it was a boy. The publishers of those paper-back thrillers used to experiment with magazines of the same intellectual level every now and then as far back as the 1880's. The idea was to reach out for that class of readers who lacked the staying power to read through an entire dime novel. A sound idea, out of which has risen a uniquely American institution; no other nation is blessed with Pulps like ours. . . .

After [World War I] the Pulps enjoyed a fabulous boom, until at the height of their vogue in 1928 some twenty million persons read them every month. All of these eager readers had to seek out the magazines and buy them on the news stands, for the Pulps

Marcus Duffield, "The Pulps: Day Dreams for the Masses," *Vanity Fair*, vol. 40, June 1933, p. 26.

never have tried to build up home subscription lists. The circulation is somewhat lower now, both because of the depression and because of the rise of the rival movie magazines. But there are still some fifty Pulps, almost any one of which has more circulation than a "quality" magazine such as *Harper's* or *Forum*.

Miners, mechanics and quick-lunch dishwashers who find life dull have only to open *Ranch Romances* to translate themselves into hard-riding cowboys beloved of man and beast, saving the herds and heroines of Bar BQ Ranch. Chicago soda-jerkers living in tenements with their mothers and three snivelling little sisters are transformed into dare-devils of the sky merely by reading *War Aces*. Girls in Pennsylvania hosiery mills and Kansas City ten-cent stores find their handsome lovers in *True Confessions*. The Pulps manufacture day-dreams, on a wholesale scale.

The Pulp Authors

The people who write Pulp stories are somewhat of a mystery even to the editors themselves, because they seldom sign their real names. It is known that one of the popular authors of science wonder stories is an assistant professor of chemistry in an eastern university. Another frequent contributor is the proprietor of a speakeasy on Park Avenue, who does not need the money but writes for the joy of it. He takes great pride in the immaculate condition of his manuscript and offers a box of candy to any sub-editor who finds an error in it. The truly professional Pulp author (often a former newspaper man) earns his living at it by grinding out from one thousand to five thousand words a day with grim regularity. Energetic writers who have caught the fancy of the Pulp public have been known to make $25,000 a year.

Since they are paid by the word, the prosperity of professional authors depends upon their speed; hence they have developed what is probably the fastest rate of literary creation in history. One favorite writer produces his stories so swiftly that the sub-editors dread having to handle them because the manuscript is so extraordinarily bad. The trouble is, he doesn't take time to read over what he has written; he is likely to get well into a sentence, forget how it started, and leave it dangling in mid-air without a verb or a predicate. The editors can tell when he interrupts a story to go to lunch because when he resumes the story he frequently has forgotten which character is which and is likely to get the hero and the villain mixed up.

This is a common mishap with Pulp writers; so common that a precautionary method has been devised by one veteran. Before starting to write a story he takes a clean sheet of paper and notes on it, for instance, "Hero; Fred Smith; red hair; brown eyes; six feet; twenty-two." Each time he introduces a new character he makes similar notes. This system, he says, practically guarantees one against the danger of referring to the villain as a short, stocky man with a gold tooth on page nine and as a tall, hawk-faced individual with porcelain uppers on page eighteen.

Tricks of the Pulp Trade

Numerous such tricks of the trade make life easier for the experienced Pulp writers, and they exchange their knowledge with a true fraternal spirit. A Kentuckian whose only nautical experience has been a ten-day wedding trip on the Great Lakes may decide to do some sea stories. Does he thereupon waste time going around the world on a freighter to get atmosphere? By no means. He writes to a confrere in New York who has published sea stories asking for a glossary of terms and a few salt-water superstitions. In return, he sends a corresponding data sheet on horse-racing so that the New York sea-story author, who may never have seen a race outside the newsreels, can make his next hero a jockey.

There is, in fact, a trade journal for Pulp authors which makes a business of supplying atmosphere. Special articles cover stage terminology, description and native phrases of Hawaii, prison patter and the language of loggers. Plot advice also is given. One seasoned fictioneer confided to his fellow Pulp authors that he had for years drawn his plots out of anecdotes in the Bible which he had put into modern dress and sold to every sex magazine printed in English.

Cookie-Cutter Fiction

The mass production of day-dreams by the Pulps has been accompanied by a phenomenon unique in literature: the standardization of fiction. Even as Fords and hairpins are standardized, so are stories. These magazines represent the incursion of the Machine Age into the art of tale-telling.

By the process of trial and error through the careers of the Pulps, definite specifications have been evolved for the various types of stories. The specifications have been formulated into a series of editorial rules, both commands and taboos, which assure the essential sameness of all the stories. Should the authors slip up, it falls to the sub-editors to enforce the taboos by revising the manuscripts.

Here is an actual incident showing how it works. A Western story magazine, hungered for "romantic adventure of the glamorous West; love is paramount but stories must be packed with cow action." A story was submitted which was brimming with cow action, was just what the magazine wanted—except that the hero, after passing through a splendid assortment of perils, was rescued in the end by three airplanes. Now, airplanes were strictly taboo in the magazine, so a sub-editor was instructed to eliminate them. He did; he changed "whirring" to "thudding," and "gleaming wings" to "foam-flecked haunches." The three airplanes became six horses and the story went to the printer.

The reason for the standardization is not to help speed the mass production—although it does enable the Pulp writers to turn out the reams of stories they do—but rather to make the yarns conform with the pattern of their readers' natural daydreams. The Pulp customers never allow social problems to intrude into their own flights of fancy; hence the magazines rigorously bar any touch of contemporary realism. Heroines never are concerned about careers, only about wedding rings; war is never disagreeable, but always a glorious adventure; and there is no Depression.

Mr. Hoover's Committee on Recent Social Trends [an attempt of the Herbert Hoover administration to understand the social condition of Americans] solemnly thumbed over a lot of Pulps looking for "attitude indicators" which would reveal approval or disapproval of such matters as old-fashioned religion and morality. The Committee noted that the Pulps were very conservative. Two hundred and thirty-three attitude indicators showed disapproval of sex relations out of wedlock, immodesty and the like, while only thirty-one attitude indicators showed approval of such laxity. This gave a twelve percent approval as compared to a thirty-five percent approval of indiscretion in the quality magazines. The Pulps also were unflagging in their enthusiasm for family life and the rearing of children, whereas the quality magazines betrayed a sharp falling off in the desire to produce offspring. In sum, the Pulps were the most moral of any magazines.

Mr. Hoover's Committee appeared a bit surprised at this conclusion. But it needn't have been, because the Pulps know what they are about. They have found that the philosophy of their readers is a synthesis of Sunday School lessons. Therefore it is by rigid editorial specification that the magazines are highly moral, so that nobody will be shocked.

The remarkable standardization extends even to the characters in the stories. The reader puts himself in the most desirable rōle, and some enemy in the least desirable; so the heroes are all good and the villains all black, and that's all there is to it. The characters need have no more individuality than so many dummies in a tailor shop.

The Pulp Heroine

Consider, for instance, the heroine in magazines like *Sweetheart Stories* or *Thrilling Love*. No matter how many different names she may bear, she is still the same pure girl in every story in every issue. She *must:*

> Be young—between 18 and 24.
> Radiate physical loveliness.
> Work for her living, earning barely enough to get by.
> Be as pure in thought as in deed.
> Win her man in lawful wedlock in the end.

> She *must not:*

> Defile her lips with nicotine.
> Have a college education.
> Touch strong drink.
> Display any sense of humor.
> Allow kisses by any but parents or fiancé.

And when the same throbbing climax comes in every story, our little heroine invariably is found panting in a genteel manner. "He had called her sweetheart—at last," recounts *Thrilling Love*. "Her lips parted a little, her breathing grew a bit more rapid. He was regarding her with a rapt, earnest expression; and as he lifted his hands to her elbows, she swayed slightly toward him.". . .

The heroes, equally stereotyped, must be as handsome as collar ad, as virile as Jack Holt, and as clean as a boy scout. Take, for instance, Robert Wallidge in a story called "Second Best": "Tall, good-looking and teeming with vitality, he was about as popular as any one man had a right to be. Blessed with an amazing fund of energy, he commanded an income rather out of keeping with his youth, as an attorney. He was a sportsman to his toes."

In the magazines that have to do with the World War, of which there are a couple of dozen, special pains are taken to make the hero impervious to fear. The verb "cry" is officially banned even as a synonym for "say". A phrase such as "'Put that down', he cried", is altered, lest the readers misunderstand, to "'Put that down,' he gritted". The hero may also rasp, grate, husk, rip or jerk whatever he has to say, so long as he never cries it.

Hairy-chested as they are, these Pulp he-men are alike in their careful avoidance of strong language. Heroes in the trenches can, under the stress of excitement, exclaim "cripes!", but must not let slip either gee or geez, which are forbidden as blasphemous. The oldest of the Western story magazines has never had its pages sullied by a Damn.

The Literary Value of Pulps

One must not be too supercilious about the Pulps. The New York Public Library, no doubt after grave consideration, has found them worthy. It buys them all. They are withheld from the casual readers, because the Library feels that its periodical room should be occupied by persons of somewhat better literary tastes. It fears, perhaps made available generally there would be no seats left for people who wanted to read, say, *The Literary Digest.* But, though hidden, the Pulps are there, and anyone with a serious purpose may have access to them. Solely out of a sense of duty to the coming generation, the Library solemnly binds and stores away the Pulps in the belief that they contain valuable sidelights on the social history of the twentieth century. Future scholars may wish to study these embalmed day-dreams to find out how the American proletariat reacted.

Federally Funded Arts

Edward Robb Ellis

A central goal of the Works Progress Administration (WPA) was to provide jobs to people in the same fields as they had worked before the Depression, and artists were not exempt. Artists were hit hard by the Depression—people considered art an extravagance they could not afford in an age when many people were barely scraping by. Artists, like all WPA employees, were given work that would serve the common good. Writers produced contemporary histories of counties and states as well as the slave narratives project, in which journalists documented the lives of former slaves. Painters created murals in public buildings, many of which you can see today in Midwestern post offices and historic buildings such as San Francisco's Coit Tower. Actors, many of whom were put out of work by both the Depression and the rising popularity of the film industry, performed plays at Civilian Conservation Corps camps. The following excerpt from Edward Robb Ellis's book, *A Nation in Torment: The Great Depression, 1929–1939*, describes the programs for artists within the WPA. Ellis's other books include *Echoes of Distant Thunder: Life in the United States, 1914–1918* and *A Diary of the Century: Tales by America's Greatest Diarist.*

The New Deal did more to promote culture than any previous administration in the history of this nation.

Critics who cried "Boondoggle!" were unaware that New Dealers were following and enhancing a precept laid down by George Washington. In his first address to the First Congress, the father of our country declared that "there is nothing which can better deserve your patronage than the promotion of science and literature." More than a century after Washington spoke these words, American civilization had become a business civilization, with art and letters and even education regarded as a luxury. [President Franklin] Roosevelt and [Harry] Hopkins, however, understood that creativity deserves as much government support as manufacturing.

Edward Robb Ellis, *A Nation in Torment: The Great Depression, 1929–1939*. New York: Kodansha International, Inc., 1995. Copyright © 1970 by Edward Robb Ellis. All rights reserved. Reproduced by permission of Coward-McCann, Inc., a division of Penguin Group (USA) Inc.

Writers and the WPA

With the advent of the Depression, unemployed men and women found themselves with unlimited leisure time, so millions of them began reading as never before in their lives. They haunted libraries, borrowed a dozen or so books at a time, kept librarians among the busiest of all people during that trying time. But few people could afford to buy their own books, and in 1930 book sales began to fall sharply. One big publishing house and four or five smaller ones went bankrupt; this meant that recognized authors lost all accrued and future royalties, while unknown writers had trouble selling their manuscripts. Several magazines suspended publication; those that managed to survive shrank to half their former size. Surprisingly, the Book-of-the-Month Club prospered during the Depression.

Robert Frost earned less than $3,000 a year each year of the decade. Norman Mailer's parents were poor. Jesse Stuart found himself penniless in 1932. With publishers less than ever willing to risk money on first novels by writers lacking a reputation, young men scribbled away without hope of being published. At a 1932 meeting of young writers in New York an older writer asked from the platform: "How do you manage to keep going?" Laughter bubbled from a corner of the hall where half a dozen poets sat with their wives. Then one of the youths got up and said: "We marry schoolteachers." Unlike Chicago, where schoolteachers often went unpaid, New York City managed to pay full salaries to its teachers in the depths of the Depression, and as a consequence, these young ladies were regarded as people of economic consequence. Most struggling writers lived off their wives or off their parents, as in the case of John Steinbeck, took odd jobs or brooded in cafeterias.

Unable to find meaningful work, ignored by society, their talents rusting, having ample time to ponder their plight, artists of all kinds—writers and painters, sculptors and musicians—began to turn radical. Harry M. Kurtzworth, a critic of the Los Angeles *Saturday Night*, questioned the glory of the artist who starves in his walk-up attic for the sake of his art. "Art flourishes only in periods of abundance," he said, "of surplus time, money, energy. Starving people have other interests." [Novelist] John Dos Passos snapped at F. Scott Fitzgerald for dwelling on a subject so trivial as his own nervous breakdown: "Christ, man, how do you find time in the middle of the general conflagration to worry about all that stuff? . . . We're living in one of the damndest tragic moments in history." During the Thirties Ernest Hemingway published only one novel, *To Have and Have Not*. Into the mouth of his dying protagonist, Harry Morgan, he put these words: "No matter how . . . a man ain't got no bloody . . . chance."

By 1935 the nation was facing the possibility of an utter collapse in the art movement. In August of that year the federal government announced that it intended to spend $27 million on a four arts division within the WPA to help musicians, actors, writers, painters, sculptors, architects, etchers, frescoists and photographers. Some businessmen grumbled. Several newspapers, though, praised this new program as humane, idealistic and farseeing.

The germ of this arts program was planted in the CWA [Civil Works Administration]. At that earlier time it had evoked rhapsodic response from Gutzon Borglum, the sculptor who carved the heads of four American Presidents in the stone face of Mount Rushmore. In a letter . . . Borglum had said:

> Mr. Hopkins' department has opened the door, a crack, but opened to this great field of human interest and thought. The world of creative impulse, without which people perish. Frankly, a people have as much right to be saved as the trees, the birds, the whole animal kingdom, and no more, but their civilization must be saved. . . .
> All there is of God in creation is what man in lonely martyrdom wrung from nowhere and everywhere, and it has been his consciousness of that that makes him master of the world, and not business or money, we must save that, civilization contains all that is precious in what we think we are. Will a basket of bread save that, a full belly and a dry back? . . . Have we in gold—the worship of Aaron's calf—made our final bow in the hall of world fame, to be remembered with Rome for our abuse of wealth?

The WPA's arts division consisted of four separate programs. As overall supervisor of them Harry Hopkins chose Jacob Baker, liberal in his tastes and a believer in experimentation. The music program was headed by Nikolai Sokoloff, conductor of the Cleveland Orchestra and a frequent guest conductor of many other symphony orchestras throughout the nation. The art program was directed by Holger Cahill, an art critic, authority on folk art and an outstanding museum technician. The theater project was headed by Hallie Flanagan. The writers' program was headed by Henry Alsberg, an editorial writer for the New York *Evening Post* and a foreign correspondent for liberal magazines.

Alsberg told Hopkins that the WPA could make a lasting cultural contribution to the nation if the men and women employed by the writers' project were put to work preparing a series of guidebooks about the states, one for each state. He pointed out that the latest issue of Baedeker's guide to America had been issued in 1909—so outdated that it advised Europeans planning to visit this land to bring along matches, buttons and dress gloves. Agreeing, Hopkins gave Alsberg the word to launch the American Guide Series.

This series revolutionized the writing of American history by presenting history in terms of communities, in relation to place. For example, the Illinois guidebook presents such a detailed and graphic study of the town of Galena that one can better understand the life of Galena's most famous hometown boy—Ulysses S. Grant.

Alsberg began hiring unemployed writers and editors, librarians and photographers, until at last he had 7,500 people at work. A director was named for each of the forty-eight states, and they, in turn, received the help of local reporters, historians, genealogists, librarians and businessmen. Each did his part in the massive chore of researching, writing, editing and publishing the state guidebooks, and soon copy was pouring into the Washington headquarters at the rate of 50,000 words a day.

[Writer and editor] Bernard De Voto spoke slightingly of the writers' program as "a project for research workers" while a New Deal critic said that only 21 percent of the people employed on the New York City project had ever written for a living. While all this may have been true, such criticism meant little because a massive literary effort of this kind required the services of skilled researchers. Besides, as Hopkins might have said, even researchers had to eat. There were also Congressmen who disliked the idea of paying money to men and women who pushed pens, and Charles D. Stewart, vice-president of the Society of Midland Authors, called the writers' project completely foolish.

Actually, it helped save the lives, sanity and talents of some writers already famous, along with others who went on to fame. In 1930 Conrad Aiken had won a Pulitzer Prize for his *Selected Poems*, but a few years later he was so badly in need of money that he joined the writers' project. Among the others on the rolls were John Cheever, Claude McKay, Vardis Fisher, Maxwell Bodenheim, Lyle Saxon, Ben A. Botkin and Edward Dahlberg—to name just a few.

They were paid an average of $90 a month. Since this was not enough to permit them to save any money, and since they were individualists, they talked from time to time about getting "a real job." Occasionally they became so disgusted that they took part in demonstrations, such as sit-ins, but the project also contained fringe benefits like the cottages the FERA [Federal Emergency Relief Act] built for authors in Florida.

Most of the nation's struggling writers lived in New York City, whose writers' project was set up on a par with state divisions. At its peak the New York City project employed more than 500 workers—writers, administrators, supervisors, photographers, mapmakers and so on. Among them was Maxwell Bodenheim, a poet and novelist of alcoholic habits and eccentric ways.

He haunted Greenwich Village, which he called "the Coney Island of the soul." One of Bodenheim's novels was *Replenishing Jessica*, the story of the promiscuous daughter of a millionaire, and it became a best seller in 1925. But with the coming of the Depression his books stopped selling. Before the creation of the writers' project, he had staggered to a city relief agency to demand help for poets. Given a $2.50 voucher for groceries, he complained that he had no home, no way to cook the groceries and was unable to eat the voucher itself. Later he was taken on the WPA project, where he did good work, but nothing could halt the death march of this self-condemned man. After the program ended Bodenheim wrote poems on scraps of paper, selling them for $1, then 50 cents, finally for 10-cent beers.

Bodenheim's life and career were not at all typical of the writers who took help from the WPA. Thanks to federal funds, they ate regularly, held up their heads pridefully and polished talents which otherwise might have eroded. Among those benefiting from this program was Richard Wright, among the first of the nation's noted black authors and finally one of its greatest.

Born on a Mississippi plantation, Wright moved to Memphis and decided to become a writer, started selling poems and stories to little magazines, moved to Chicago where he joined the writers' project, pushed on to New York in 1937 and went to work for the project in that city. He wrote the essay on Harlem for the WPA book called *New York Panorama*. In 1939 he won a Guggenheim Fellowship, which enabled him to quit the project and finish his novel *Native Son*, picked by the Book-of-the-Month Club as one of its 1940 selections.

Tennessee Williams failed in his effort to get on the writers' project. When he was about twenty-two, he scraped up enough money to take a train from St. Louis to Chicago, where he tried desperately to join the WPA. Of this experience, he later wrote: "My work lacked 'social content' or 'protest' and I couldn't prove that my family was destitute and I still had, in those days, a touch of refinement in my social behavior which made me seem frivolous . . . to the conscientiously rough-hewn pillars of the Chicago project." He later applied to the theater project but was turned down again, largely because of his family's relative affluence.

One of the greatest accomplishments of the writers' project was its historical records survey, instituted in 1936. Relief workers took inventories of local public records stored in city hall cellars, library lofts and court house garrets. They indexed old newspaper files. They made abstracts of court cases containing nuggets of local history. They examined business archives, looked through church records, studied tombstones to verify vital statistics. The perfection of microfilm had made it possible for them to photograph, and thus to preserve, millions of pages crumbling into decay. They measured, sketched, diagrammed and photographed 2,300 historic buildings.

In 1937 the American Guide Series became a reality with publication of the first of the set, a book about Idaho. By the end of its life the project produced 378 books and pamphlets—a volume for each of the forty-eight states, 30 about our major cities, others about historic waterways and highways, such as *The Oregon Trail*. Various commercial and university publishers issued these works, with royalties either paying for everything except labor costs or going into the federal treasury.

In a *New Republic* article Robert Cantwell said of the writers' project: "The least publicized of the art projects, it may emerge as the most influential and valuable of them all." Nearly one-third of a century later the American Guide Series continued to be a prime source of information for every serious writer of American history.

Musicians and the WPA

Musicians were suffering even before the beginning of the Depression. The popularity of radio, the advent of talking movies and the death of vaudeville had thrown 50,000 musical performers out of work. After the Crash there were few Americans who could afford music lessons for their children, so music teachers lost their pupils or had to cut their fees for the few who remained. Music publishers, recording companies and manufacturers of musical instruments earned less or suffered heavy losses. To most of these people the federal music project, under Nikolai Sokoloff, came as salvation.

Established in July, 1935, the music program put musicians to work in orchestras and bands, in chamber music and choral and operatic groups throughout the nation. Forty-five cities obtained their own WPA symphony orchestra, while 110 other cities got orchestras with more than thirty-five players. Just before the start of a concert by a WPA orchestra in Florida, a violinist apologized to the audience on behalf of his colleagues and himself for the quality of their concert. He explained that their fingers were stiff because of their previous relief job—working on a road gang.

When the music project was at its peak it supported 15,000 people. They gave a total of 150,000 programs heard by more than 100,000,000 people, many of whom had been unfamiliar with anything but popular songs. Each month more than 500,000 pupils attended free music classes. WPA musical groups relieved the boredom of hospital patients. Project workers dug out and recorded American folk music—the Cajun songs of Louisiana, the Indian-flavored songs of early Oklahoma, the British-born ballads of Kentucky mountaineers, the African-inspired songs of Mississippi bayous.

Although the program was designed to help performers more than composers, since the former outnumbered latter, it established a composers' forum-laboratory. Before the project was terminated, 1,400 native composers produced 4,915 original compositions—some bad, many mediocre, a few hailed by music critics as "distinguished." One prominent critic, Deems Taylor, wrote in 1935: "It is safe to say that during the past two years the WPA orchestras alone have probably performed more American music than our other symphony orchestras, combined, during the past ten."

Thanks to this project, music became democratized in this country. In about the year 1915 there had been only 17 symphony orchestras in the United States; by 1939 there were more than 270. Europe's leadership in the musical world, together with its snobbish aloofness, had been shattered.

The WPA Art Project

The WPA art project was set up by Holger Cahill on "the principle that it is not the solitary genius but a sound general movement which maintains art as a vital, functioning part of any cultural scheme."

All a person had to do to get on the art project was to obtain proof from local authorities that he needed relief and that he had once had some connection, however tenuous, with the world of art. As a result, of the more than 5,000 people ultimately hired, fewer than half ever painted a picture, sculpted a statue or decorated a building with a mural. This does not mean that the art program was a boondoggle. While creativity flowered among the great artists—Jackson Pollock, Aaron Bohrod, Ben Shahn, Willem de Kooning, Concetta Scaravaglione, Anna Walinska and the like—those with limited talent taught free art classes, photographed historic houses, painted posters and designed stage sets for the federal theater project. Others maintained sixty-six community art centers which attracted a total of 6,000,000 visitors.

In addition to the invaluable and enduring artworks produced by the most gifted relief workers, the art project left all of us a monumental *Index of American Design*. This part of the program was directed by Constance Rourke and gave employment to about 1,000 artists. Wishing to find and preserve specimens of early American arts and crafts, they ransacked New England farmhouses, museums, antique shops, historical societies, Shaker barns and California missions. They photographed or painted every treasure they discovered—embroidered seat covers, oil paintings, watercolors, carved figureheads, antique quilts and samplers, weather vanes and such. Collectively, these artists produced 7,000 illustrations of every variety of native American art.

WPA Theater

On May 16, 1935, the phone rang in the Poughkeepsie, New York, home of a small, red-headed middle-aged woman named Hallie Flanagan. When she answered it, she heard Jacob Baker, the head of the WPA's four arts program, saying that he was calling from Washington. "Mr. Hopkins wants you to come to Washington to talk about unemployed actors," Baker said. Miss Flanagan was in charge of Vassar College's Experimental Theatre. She knew Hopkins, for they had grown up together in Grinnell, Iowa, and attended the same college.

Over the wire she said to Baker, probingly: "Mr. Hopkins knows, of course, that my theater here is a non-commercial one—that I'm not connected with the commercial theater?"

"Yes, he knows that. He's conferring with commercial theater people, too. There are dozens of theater people down here. Mr. Hopkins wants to see you. Can you come?"

She went to Washington, rode the shaky elevator in the Walker-Johnson Building, walked into Hopkins' plain office. Grinning at her, he said the government was about to establish a federal theater project and he wanted her to take charge of it.

"This is a tough job we're asking you to do," he added. "I don't know why I still hang onto the idea that unemployed actors get just as hungry as anybody else."

She accepted the job, and a few days later Hopkins posed a curious question: "Can you spend money?"

Miss Flanagan confessed that the inability to spend money was not one of her faults.

But Hopkins was serious. "It's not easy," he told her. "It takes a lot of nerve to put your signature down on a piece of paper, when it means that the government of the United States is going to pay out a million dollars to the unemployed in Chicago. It takes decision—because you'll have to decide whether Chicago needs that money more than New York City or Los Angeles."

Actors, as Miss Flanagan knew, were suffering severe hardships. Like musicians, many had lost their jobs with the death of vaudeville and the birth of the talkies. No one knew for sure just how many performers were out of work. Actors Equity said there were 5,000 unemployed actors in New York City alone, while WPA officials put the nationwide total at 20,000 to 30,000 people. In Harlem black entertainers were kissing the Tree of Hope, a local talisman, for luck.

In 1931 two-thirds of Manhattan's playhouses were shut. During the 1932–33 season eight out of every ten new plays failed. . . . In 1932 no less than 22,000 people registered with Hollywood casting bureaus. *Variety* had reduced its price from 25 to 15 cents. Some film stars still commanded huge salaries but fearfully had taken out kidnap insurance policies with Lloyd's of London. With the rise of [Nazi leader Adolf] Hitler in Germany and [Dictator Benito] Mussolini in Italy, thousands of foreign actors—many of them Jewish—had fled to the United States, where they now sought work. The American Federation of Actors was planning to stage circuses to aid those of its members who were broke and hungry.

On July 27, 1935, Miss Flanagan was sworn in as administrator of the new federal theater project. The ceremony was held in a Washington playhouse called the old Auditorium, a vast hulk of a building now abuzz with rushing people, whirring electric fans, riveting machines and cement-slapping plasterers. She sat down in a new cubicle and conferred with her staff of four about the possibility of getting at least 10,000 theater people back to work within a short time.

Since Broadway was the heart of the American theater, Miss Flanagan wanted an especially able man to direct the New York City unit of her project, and her choice was Elmer Rice. The forty-three-year-old Rice had proved himself as a playwright, stage director and novelist. With the deepening of the Depression, his plays had shifted from realistic reporting to social and political themes. Rice already had sent Hopkins a letter outlining a plan for the establishment of a national theater, but he hesitated about accepting Miss Flanagan's offer because he was about to begin writing another novel.

"What could we do with all the actors?" he asked her. "Even

if we had twenty plays in rehearsal at once, with thirty in a cast, that would keep only a fraction of them busy."

Badly wanting Rice, she grabbed at a straw and impulsively said: "We wouldn't use them all in plays, We could do *Living Newspapers*. We could dramatize the news with living actors, light, music, movement."

This idea appealed to Rice, who cried: "Yes! And I can get the Newspaper Guild to back it!"

Before taking the job, though, Rice got a promise from Hopkins that there would be no censorship and that he would have no superior but Miss Flanagan. Then he set up headquarters in an abandoned bank on Eighth Avenue. Everything had to be started from scratch. One day Rice asked an assistant, whom he regarded as "a dreary little civil servant," for pencils, writing tablets and paper clips. This helper said they would have to be requisitioned. Rice curtly told him to go ahead and requisition them. His assistant said: "First we'll have to requisition some requisition blanks."

Elmer Rice was paid $260 a month on the theory that he worked thirteen days at $20 a day, but actually he worked from early morning until late at night every day of the month, including Sundays. It amused him to get nasty letters accusing him of making a fortune on a soft government job. Sometimes he opened press conferences by saying to reporters: "Well, what do you vultures want to swoop down on now?"

At first jobs were limited to entertainers on home relief rolls, but this excluded many who had been too proud to ask for help. Miss Flanagan and Rice managed to get this rule modified. She watched in horror as a man applying for work went mad and beat his head against a wall. A famous clown was taken on the WPA rolls, became so excited at the chance to work again that on the opening night of the show he suffered a stroke from which he never recovered.

Rice issued this statement:

> The Federal Theatre Project has been created for the purpose of providing worthwhile employment for professional theatre workers. Please bear in mind that you are not being offered relief or charity but WORK. The interviewers have been instructed to receive you with the same courtesy and consideration that would

be extended by any professional employment agency, our object being to set up so high a standard of professional excellence in these projects that they will be able to continue on their own momentum after the federal program is completed.

Into the project flocked young men and women who later became celebrated actors—Joseph Cotton, Orson Welles, Arthur Kennedy, Burt Lancaster, Arlene Francis, Ed Gardner, Rex Ingram, Canada Lee, Howard da Silva, William Bendix, Bil Baird. Another employed by the WPA, but not on the theater project, was Robert Ryan, who worked as a paving supervisor.

At its peak the program gave work to 12,700 theater people in twenty-nine states. Besides the actors themselves, there were producers, directors, playwrights, stagehands, electricians, propmen—all the crafts found in stage work. Hopkins had told Miss Flanagan: "We're for labor—first, last and all the time. WPA is labor—don't forget that." He insisted that $9 of every $10 be spent on wages, leaving only about $1 to meet operating costs. Nine out of every 10 people hired had to come from relief rolls. Wages averaged $83 a month, although some actors were paid up to $103.40 a month for performing in New York City. According to the place and circumstance, admission to WPA shows was free, or cost 10 cents, 25 cents, 50 cents, and in rare instances as much as $1.

The federal theater project presented many different kinds of shows—Negro drama, dance drama, children's theater, puppet and marionette shows, a documentary about syphilis, classical drama, modern drama, foreign language drama, musicals, Living Newspapers, pageants, vaudeville, circus, religious drama, spectacles, opera and radio programs.

Leisure and Entertainment

CHAPTER
3

Chapter Preface

The ways in which people entertained themselves during the Great Depression were in many ways reflections of the Depression itself. At home, people played board games such as Monopoly and listened to radio programs such as *Little Orphan Annie*, which reflected the contrast between the wealthy and the poor and had as their theme a chance to become miraculously rich. Beginning in 1933, each Sunday night President Franklin Roosevelt delivered radio broadcasts called Fireside Chats to the American people, which reflected a personal relationship between the president and the people's suffering.

Purveyors of public entertainment had to adapt to keep in business. Movie theaters lowered ticket prices, showed double features, and sponsored raffles. Dance marathons offered couples a chance to win money. If they were willing to stand, people could attend the racetrack and bet a few pennies on their favorite horse.

The following chapter describes some of the ways that people tried to escape from hardship, distract themselves from their difficulties, and have some fun during the Great Depression.

Escaping to the Movies

Robert Sklar

Escape from the difficulties of life helped keep up the hopes and spirits of those who lived through the Great Depression, and Hollywood films provided such means of escape. By devoting part of their scarce income to going to the movies, people were able to experience the glamour, romance, adventure, and excitement that was lacking in their own lives. The Marx Brothers made people laugh; *Frankenstein* and *King Kong* frightened and thrilled, and children who were denied a carefree childhood lived one vicariously through Shirley Temple. The following excerpt from Robert Sklar's *Film: An International History of the Medium* describes some of the films and genres that defined the times and are now recognized as classics. Sklar is a professor of cinema studies at New York University.

When talk about the movies turns ethereal—when words like magic and myth, glamour and legend crop up—it immediately evokes, for most people, images from 1930s Hollywood. [Fred] Astaire and [Ginger] Rogers airborne in a dance step. [Greta] Garbo in a lover's embrace. Judy Garland, as Dorothy, and her little dog Toto on the yellow brick road. [Cary] Grant and [Katharine] Hepburn chasing a leopard through Connecticut. These and scores of similar scenes from American films of the 1930s are almost invariably the associations that come to mind when we think of movies not only as enormously successful mass entertainment but as creators of a style of living— of dressing, of speaking, of romancing—that affected people throughout the world, and continues to exert its power.

Yet the world of images that Hollywood constructed—the magical and glamorous part of it, at any rate—was far removed from the surrounding world of actuality. The 1930s began with the most severe economic depression of the century and ended with the outbreak of a devastating world war. American motion picture companies were affected by these disruptions as were all institutions and peoples. Nearly all the Hollywood studios suffered financial losses during the Great Depression, which struck soon after the companies had borrowed substantial sums to finance the conversion to sound. Paramount, Fox, and RKO were among the firms whose management was temporarily controlled by courts, banks, or other debt-holders, while filmmaking policies generally continued in the hands of experienced studio executives. The studios were further challenged during the period by accusations against the morality of their films and the legality of their business practices.

The Dream Machine

Still, the Hollywood "dream machine" functioned smoothly in the public's eyes; its attraction during an era of social and political crisis can surely be explained by spectators' desires to "escape" for a few hours their own and the world's troubles into a make-believe place where happy endings were the rule. But that wish is not limited just to the 1930s. More specific to the era were the growth of mass society and the increasing cultural importance of popular commercial entertainment. Though movies had demonstrated wide appeal in earlier decades, particularly among young people, the arrival of sound films, coupled with a crisis in traditional values caused by the depression's impact on the economy and social life, catapulted the film industry to a position of acknowledged cultural power it had not possessed before.

New Talent

Talking pictures—and later, political repression overseas—also brought to Hollywood new waves of creative and technical talent. The need for dialogue lured across the continent playwrights, journalists, novelists, stage performers, and directors to motion picture work; prominent examples includes director George Cukor (1899–1983); writer-director Preston Sturges (1898–1959), and performers Paul Muni (1895–1967) and Katharine Hepburn [1907–2003]. In Germany, meanwhile, the rise of the fascist Nazi movement to political power sent many of that country's leading film personnel into exile, some elsewhere in Europe, many to the United States. The presence in Southern California of refugee artists in such other fields as literature and music helped to turn the once-isolated movie "colony" into a center where some of the outstanding American and European figures in the literary and visual arts turned their hands to the popular art of American movies. . . .

The Star System

The profession most affected by the advent of talkies, quite obviously, was acting. Nearly every studio added several dozen stage-trained players to its roster during 1929–30; many flopped, but a few quickly became stars, including Spencer Tracy (1900–1967) at Fox, Irene Dunne (1898–1990) at RKO, and James Cagney (1899–1986) at Warner Bros. The arrival of so many new performers brought changes in [what is called] the star system. With beginning players, starting from scratch, the studios sought to gain firmer control over careers and salaries than in the 1920s, when stars' salaries had soared and a few had gained considerable power to approve scripts and casting decisions. As the sound era began, virtually every aspirant for leading roles was obliged to become a "contract player" with a specific studio; only later in the 1930s did a few outstanding stars, such as Barbara Stanwyck (1907–1990) and Cary Grant (1904–1986), strike out on their own as successful "free-lancers."

The host of stage players who came to Hollywood signed contracts that by theater standards were generous, and to the average persona fortune, but by previous Hollywood norms the salaries were a mere pittance. As contract players they were generally bound for up to seven years, but the studios had frequent "options" to drop them before the contract expired. They could be loaned out to other studios (at a profit to their employer) and suspended without pay if they refused a role. The studios shaped their public images through publicity staffs who orchestrated coverage in the press and fan magazines and leaked items (not always favorable, if performers were making trouble or about to be dropped) to gossip columnists. This form of "grooming" often had little to do with actual development of screen performance; in practice, contract players outnumbered good roles, and the production system depended on the repetition of character types rather than individuated performances. Any contract player who broke through to become a star, though well recompensed by any standard, was nevertheless grossly underpaid in terms of box office value to the studio, and not even the highest-paid stars of the 1930s earned salaries comparable to what leading stars had been paid in silent days.

The Classical Era

The developing star system of the 1930s marks one of the key elements of what has frequently been called the classical era of Hollywood cinema. As applied to the American film industry, "classic" and "classical" are loose terms with several meanings and periodizations. Most fundamentally they refer to the mode of production and aesthetic styles fostered by the vertically integrated studios—those controlling not only production but also distribution and exhibition—that took shape in the 1910s and operated until the 1950s. . . .

Perhaps the key word for American movies in this era is adaptability. The major companies and most of their important personnel weathered the changeover to talkies. They survived the Great Depression. As the 1930s went on, they rode the wave of an expanding popular commercial culture to greater profits, popularity, and social influence. Since the 1930s, subsequent waves have carried American motion pictures to both new depths and new heights. But at no other time in their history have movies played so pervasive and significant a role in cultural definition and consciousness. That is a major reason why the myths and legends of the 1930s remain so vivid.

Genre Developments

The impact of sound on Hollywood's genre system, as with everything else, was contradictory. Things stayed the same and things became different. Few if any of the dominant silent film genres were adversely affected by the advent of talkies. Conversely, few if any new genres were inaugurated as a result of sound (the one major exception was the musical with recorded sound; it drove out the staged musical prologues that had been an important exhibition feature in the silent period). There were developments within genres, to be sure, but in general these derived as much from cultural and industrial factors as from new technologies; the principal exception was comedy, where sound technology mingled with cultural changes to shape a new, highly verbal comedy style.

Gangster Films

The gangster genre, for example, responded significantly in the early 1930s to an increased public concern about crime and to an emerging literary treatment of legendary gang leaders of the Prohibition era. At least two dozen gangster pictures appeared in 1930, capped by the First National production *Little Caesar*, directed by Mervyn LeRoy (1900–1987). It was followed the next year by *The Public Enemy*, a Warner Bros. picture directed by William A. Wellman, and in 1932 by *Scarface*, a Howard Hughes film directed by Howard Hawks (1896–1977). Together these comprise the trio of works that has defined over the decades the early depression era gangster film.

All three films aroused strong public controversy. Reviewers and moralists were concerned about the graphic depiction of violence, as well as the possibility that powerful performances could turn fictional criminals into romantic heroes, whatever their violent fates. Each work indeed offered powerful performances in their gangster roles, launching three stage actors toward major movie careers, Edward G. Robinson (1893–1973), played Rico Bandello in *Little Caesar*, James Cagney was Tom Powers in *The Public Enemy*, and Paul Muni portrayed Tony Camonte in *Scarface*. . . .

Horror Films

The horror genre also surged in popular appeal in the early 1930s. Should we attempt to characterize spectator identification with movie monsters? The actor Lon Chaney had dominated Hollywood horror films in the 1920s with his remarkable array of makeup and disguises. With Chaney's untimely death in August 1930, at forty-seven, after making only one sound film, the genre was open to new directions in the talkie era. What was perhaps most unusual about the first of the classic sound horror films—*Dracula* (1931), a Universal production directed by Tod Browning (1880–1962)—was that the vampire, far from being as grotesque as Murnau's *Nosferatu*, looked quite normal. As played by the Hungarian actor Bela Lugosi (1882–1956), the fiend's otherworldly character was emphasized by lighting his eyes while leaving the rest of his face in shadow and by his heavy middle-European accent, which became the stock-in-trade of a thousand imitators delivering such legendary lines as "I never drink . . . wine."

Universal followed this success later the same year with *Franken-*

The movies were a favorite form of escape during the Great Depression, offering a few hours away from a difficult life.

stein, directed by James Whale (1889–1957). Its title credits were preceded by a filmed segment showing a man stepping out from stage curtains to deliver a "friendly warning": "I think it will thrill you. It may shock you. It might even *horrify* you." The performer of the monster role was identified in the opening credits with a question mark, and only at the end was the fabled figure with the flat-top head, plugs in the neck, and sewn-together body revealed to be Boris Karloff (1887–1969), a journeyman British actor who henceforth would be a fixture of the horror genre. . . .

The Musical

By the early 1930s the new genre of recorded sound musicals had already gone through one cycle, and its staying power seemed uncertain. With the exception of *Applause* and a few others, early sound musicals had been hampered by restricted camera movement and the variety format taken over from stage musicals. The genre made a decisive recovery when Warner Bros, inaugurated in 1933 a series of musicals with show-business stories featuring dances and ensemble staging created by choreographer Busby Berkeley (1895–1976).

The first, *42nd Street*, directed by Lloyd Bacon (1890–1955), told the classic tale of the "raw kid out of the chorus" who gets her big chance when the leading lady breaks her ankle. "You're going out a youngster," says the director to young Peggy Sawyer (played by Ruby Keeler), "but you've got to come back a star." Besides such familiar, but compelling, stories, the Warner musicals gave free reign to Berkeley's dance spectacles. He completely freed the musical from adherence to stage conventions; having tried out overhead shots of dancers in several earlier musicals, he advanced this style in *42nd Street*, and it reached full flower in such films as *Gold Diggers of 1933* and *Footlight Parade* (both 1933) and *Dames* (1934). *42nd Street* also offers a tracking shot with a male vocalist while the camera passes between the legs of female dancers. These and similar images from other films have made Berkeley's dances prime subjects for studies concerned with the mechanization, objectification, and segmentation of women's bodies in cinema.

Almost simultaneously with Berkeley's triumphs, a different musical style, which placed a more contemplative emphasis on individual performances, was emerging in the Fred Astaire (1899–1987) and Ginger Rogers (b. 1911) musicals made at RKO. (Rogers personified the transition, having appeared in *42nd Street* and *Gold Diggers of 1933*). Fred and Ginger—we seem to know no other Hollywood couple so familiarly on a first-name basis—danced together in nine films between 1933 and 1939, to music by Cole Porter, Irving Berlin, Jerome Kern, George Gershwin, and other leading popular composers, with dance direction by Hermes Pan (1905–1990). Their most prominent successes (and enduring favorites) included *Top Hat* (1935), directed by Mark Sandrich (1900–1945), and *Swing Time* (1937), directed by George Stevens (1904–1975).

Comedy

Last in this brief survey of genres, comedy received a strong boost from new writers and performers who came in with sound. Representative among the former was playwright Samson Raphaelson (1896–1983), whose stage play served as source for *The Jazz Singer;* Raphaelson brought his sardonic dialogue to director Ernst Lubitsch's sophisticated comedies twitting European upper-class society, notably *Trouble in Paradise* (1932), a Paramount film featuring Miriam Hopkins, Kay Francis, and Herbert Marshall. Inimitable among the latter was the vaudeville and Broadway comedy team the Marx Brothers (Groucho, Harpo, Chico, and Zeppo). The five anarchic comedies they made for Paramount—*The Cocoanuts* (1929) and *Animal Crackers* (1930), produced at the New York Astoria studio; then, in Hollywood, *Monkey Business* (1931), *Horse Feathers* (1932), and *Duck Soup* (1933)—remain popular favorites, though deeply rooted in the ethnic humor style of their times. . . .

An Establishment Cinema

In the space of half a decade, Hollywood had gone from something of an outlaw cinema, in the eyes of some, to something of an establishment cinema. As the United States struggled to recover from the Great Depression, as the rise of European Fascism and the onset of war caused the nation to reconsider its history and values, the movies became increasingly important as framers of cultural and ideological discourses.

The Invention of Monopoly®

Maxine Brady

During the Depression, people had to find inexpensive ways to entertain themselves at home. Board games became a popular pastime for those who could no longer afford to go out on the town in the evenings. At the same time, many unemployed people also attempted to make a living by gambling or by inventing something that would bring them wealth. This combination led to the invention of two of the country's most popular board games: Scrabble®, invented by an unemployed architect named Alfred Butts, and Monopoly. The following excerpt by Maxine Brady is a brief history of Monopoly and the man behind it, Charles Darrow. Brady is the author of *The Monopoly Book*, *Bloomingdale's: The Biography of a Store* and a contributor to *How to Get Rich with a 1-800 Number*.

The stock market crash of 1929 caused mass unemployment for millions of Americans. For Charles Darrow, the financial problems grew increasingly difficult. Once a salesman of heating and engineering equipment, he spent the early 1930s looking for a job. He'd been feeding himself, his wife, and their son by taking any odd job he could find. He repaired electric irons, did occasional fix-it jobs, even walked dogs—when he could find someone to pay him for his labors.

It wasn't enough, though. Now his wife was expecting their second child. He had to find a way to make more money.

To fill his many idle hours, and help him forget his worries temporarily, Darrow invented things. Some of them were fun; others were probably devised in hopes that they would become profitable. He made jigsaw puzzles; he created a combination bat-and-ball, which was supposed to be used as a beach toy; he designed an improved pad for recording and scoring bridge games. They were interesting diversions, but nobody was willing to pay for them.

Darrow's problem, of course, was not unique. Many of his friends and family were out of jobs, and were having trouble affording even such necessities as food and shelter. For them, as for most people, the movies, the theater, and any form of entertainment which cost any money at all was too expensive.

So they got together in the evenings and on weekends, when the offices of the Federal Emergency Relief Administration were closed, and they talked. And after the gloomy recital of that day's particular troubles, the conversation would usually become nostalgic: remember the good old days?

Darrow did. For him and his wife, thinking back to the more prosperous life they had led only a few years before, some of the pleasantest memories were of the vacations they had spent at one of their favorite holiday places, a seaside resort in New Jersey called Atlantic City.

The First Monopoly Board

One evening in 1930, Darrow sat down at his kitchen table in Germantown, Pennsylvania, and sketched out some of the street names of Atlantic City on the round piece of oilcloth that covered the table. The streets he chose were all from the same side of the city: between the Inlet and Park Place, along the Boardwalk. When he finished, Darrow was short one name, so he choose Marven Gardens, a section from nearby Margate. Probably unintentionally, he altered the spelling, and it was penciled onto his board as Marvin Gardens.

He included the three railroads that carried the wealthy vacationers to the resort, and the utility companies that serviced them, as well as the parcels of real estate of varying prices. He wanted a fourth railroad to make his board symmetrical, so he added the Short Line: actually it was a freight-carrying bus company that had a depot in Atlantic City. A local paint store gave him free samples of several colors, and he used them to color his game board. A new game began to take form in his mind.

Darrow cut houses and hotels for his little city, using scraps of wooden molding that a lumber yard had discarded. He rounded up stray pieces of cardboard, and typed out title cards for the different properties. The rest of the equipment was fairly easy to acquire; colored buttons for the tokens, a pair of dice, and a lot of play money.

From then on, in the evenings, the Darrows would sit around the kitchen table buying, renting, developing, and selling real estate. They had little enough real cash on hand, yet The Game, as they all referred to it, permitted them to manipulate large sums of money as they engaged in complex negotiations to acquire valuable blocks of property. The simple, almost crude set exerted a continuing fascination and challenge. As friends dropped in to visit, they were invited to join the game. Soon the "Monopoly evenings" became a standard feature at the Darrow home.

Popularity Increases

Then the friends wanted to take the game home with them. Each night's winner, a bit heady with his success in the nether reaches of high finance, asked for a set of his own, so that he could show off his financial wizardry. The runner-up, convinced that he could win the next time if he could only hone his skill with a little practice, generally wanted a set too. Darrow had an overabundance of free time, so he began making copies of his board, property cards, and buildings. His delighted friends supplied their own dice and tokens, and often their own package of play money.

But the demand increased, and Darrow increased his output to two handmade sets a day. Selling them for $4 apiece, each set brought him new customers. People kept talking about the new game and playing it with their friends. Through word-of-mouth advertising alone, Darrow sold about one hundred sets, and had orders for many more. But his one-at-a-time production technique simply couldn't keep up with the demand.

Encouraged by his friends, Darrow decided to test the game outside his personal sphere of acquaintances and friends of friends. He made up a few sets and offered them to department stores in Philadelphia, the nearest city. They sold.

With the knowledge that his game was marketable, he attempted to increase his rate of production. A friend helped out by printing the Monopoly boards and the title cards. Darrow continued to paint in the colors and assemble the sets by hand. This partial automation enabled him to produce six games a day. It wasn't enough.

Demand Exceeds Supply

By 1934, now fully aware that his interesting diversion had turned into a potentially profitable business, Darrow arranged to have the same friend print and package the complete sets. It looked like they had the problem solved, for a little while. Production was finally keeping pace with sales. But they hadn't reckoned with the Philadelphia sales. Soon, a department store began ordering sets wholesale, in quantities far greater than anything they could accommodate. It became obvious to Darrow that he had only two choices. He could borrow money and plunge wholeheartedly into the game business, or he could sell Monopoly to an established game company. Darrow wrote to Parker Brothers, then as now one of the world's major game manufacturers and distributors, to see if the company would be interested in producing and marketing the game on a national basis.

Parker Brothers had by then been in business for half a century, and had become accustomed to enthusiastic inventors sending in new game creations. Some of the ideas had even proven marketable, but, by and large, the company's managers tended to trust the creativity of their own staff far more than they did an unproven novice.

Although Parker Brothers thought the basic framework of the game seemed possibly interesting, they handled the game routinely. Various members of the company sat down at their offices in Salem, Massachusetts, to try it out, as they do all prospective games. They played it several times and found that they all enjoyed it. But the company had evolved a set of inviolable ground rules for "family games," which they held to be mandatory for any game that could be successfully marketed. According to the Parker precept, a family game should last approximately forty-five minutes. Monopoly could go on for hours. Parker also felt that a game should have a specific end, a goal to be achieved. (In their other board games, the players' tokens progressed around a track until they reached the end—which might be symbolized by a pot of gold, a home port, a jackpot, or even Heaven—and the first player to reach this goal was the winner.) In Monopoly, the players just kept going round and round the board. The only goal was to bankrupt the other players and emerge still solvent yourself. Furthermore, Monopoly's rules seemed far too complex to the Parker staff; they thought the general game-playing public would be hopelessly confused trying to learn how to handle mortgages, rents, and interest.

Parker Brothers Rejects the Game

After testing the game for several weeks, Parker Brothers made the unanimous decision to reject it. The company wrote and informed Darrow of this decision, explaining that his game contained "fifty-two fundamental errors." It would never be accepted by the public.

Darrow, of course, was considerably annoyed. He knew very well how people responded to his game. Despite Parker Brothers' analysis, Monopoly was decidedly marketable. Unfortunately, however, it was far more marketable than Darrow himself; he was still unemployed. Monopoly, it seemed, was virtually his only asset.

Therefore, he went back to his printer friend, ordered the production of five thousand sets, and continued to sell the game locally. But locally included Philadelphia, and the department stores there were soon aware that Darrow was increasing his output. They began placing massive orders for the Christmas season. Darrow now found himself working fourteen hours a day just trying to keep up with the shipping.

With the game now being ordered in wholesale lots, Parker's sales representatives soon became acutely aware that the Philadelphia stores were expecting huge sales of Monopoly the following Christmas, the traditional game-buying season. Word was quickly passed back to corporate headquarters in Salem, where the issue was deemed worthy of reconsideration. Then, to top things off, a major New York toy and game store, the prestigious F.A.O. Schwarz, bought two hundred sets out of the original five thousand printing.

Parker Brothers Reconsiders

Shortly afterwards, a friend telephoned Sally Barton (daughter of Parker Brothers' founder, George Parker) to rave about a wonderful new game she had purchased at F.A.O. Schwarz. It was called Monopoly, and it was hard to come by and in short supply. The friend suggested that Mrs. Barton tell Parker Brothers about it. Sally did. She told her husband, Robert B.M. Barton, who happened to be the president of the company. Curious about a competitor's product, he purchased a copy of the game at F.A.O. Schwarz, took it home and wound up playing it until 1 A.M. The next day, Barton wrote to Darrow, and three days later they met at Parker Brothers' New York sales office in the Flatiron Building.

Parker Brothers offered to buy the game outright and give Darrow royalties on all sets sold. The company insisted, though, on making some revisions which would refine the game and clarify the rules. Some of the staff were still concerned about the indefinite playing time, so they agreed to market the original version as long as Darrow permitted them to develop a variation of the game which could be played in less time. This shorter version was to be printed along with the general rules, to give the public an option.

Darrow agreed and the contract was signed. Later, in explaining why he had decided to sell his brainchild, Darrow related his decision to the monetary commitment he would have otherwise had to make in order to keep producing the game himself. "Taking the precepts of Monopoly to heart," he said, "I did not care to speculate." Years afterward, commenting on the final offer from Parker Brothers, he wrote: "I gladly accepted and have never regretted that decision."

A Happy Ending for Darrow

The royalties from sales of Monopoly soon made Darrow a millionaire. He retired at the age of forty-six, to become a gentleman farmer in Bucks County, Pennsylvania, a world traveler with a particular interest in ancient cities, a motion picture photographer, and a collector of exotic orchid species. In 1970, a few years after Darrow's death, Atlantic City erected a commemorative plaque in his honor. It stands on the Boardwalk, near the juncture of Park Place.

Baseball: The National Pastime

Charles C. Alexander

Professional baseball, like many industries, suffered during the Great Depression. Despite the lure of stars such as Babe Ruth and Lou Gehrig, widespread unemployment put the price of a stadium ticket out of reach for many, and teams played to smaller and smaller crowds. There were many "firsts" in baseball during the thirties, all efforts to keep the professional leagues alive: Radio stations broadcast live play-by-plays of games for the first time, which broadened baseball's audience; stadiums were lit, making night baseball possible for the first time; and the very first all-star game was played. One thing that did not change was the segregation of the sport: The Negro leagues remained separate from the white leagues.

In the following excerpt from *Breaking the Slump: Baseball in the Depression Era*, author Charles C. Alexander describes the baseball industry during the Depression years and what the game meant to the players and the American people. Alexander is a professor of history at Ohio University.

While the prosperous times most Americans had enjoyed for the past several years were clearly over by mid-1930 and many minor leagues were in financial trouble, the Great Depression worked a delayed reaction on big-league baseball. In 1930 attendance in the majors reached an all-time peak of about 10.1 million, but from then on the hard times that had already hit most other segments of the economy caught up with all of baseball. The early thirties brought sparse crowds, deficits, a dramatic contraction in minor-league operations, and relentless retrenchment throughout the baseball business. Major-league attendance revived considerably starting in 1934 and 1935, and largely as a result of a general conversion to nighttime baseball, the minors experienced a strong comeback. But the decade as a whole—up until the national economy began to gear up for U.S. participation in another world war—was one of hard times for what had long been hailed as America's National Pastime.

Still the National Pastime

Yet for all its difficulties in the Depression era, baseball did hold its place as the National Pastime. From the time spring training got under way in the belt of states from Florida to southern California until the conclusion of the annual World Series in October, baseball was the sport more people watched, listened to on radio, read about, and argued over than any other—probably more than all the others combined.

With a following that did not extend far from a few northeastern and midwestern cities, professional football struggled to gain a solid financial footing and build a national fandom, while professional basketball consisted of a few traveling teams and a few company-sponsored industrial leagues. Tennis and golf were still dominated by nonprofessionals; both remained basically elite sports, lacking mass followings. Prizefighting, while occasionally generating huge interest, especially for heavyweight championship bouts, had never shaken free of its bloodsport and underworld associations. College basketball was still distinctly smalltime (the National College Athletic Association didn't stage a championship tournament until the late 1930s), and college football, if supreme on campuses, nonetheless flourished in an environment that remained inaccessible to most Americans. So even though other sports would increasingly encroach on baseball's popularity with the sports-minded public, at the end of a decade of hard times baseball remained Americans' favorite form of athletic competition.

Segregation and Baseball

That was true as much for black Americans as for whites. Yet throughout its history, baseball had closely reflected dominant American social values and practices, both good and bad. And throughout the 1930s, baseball, like the larger society, remained sharply divided according to color and racial ancestry. What social commentators termed the "color line" and black citizens commonly called "Jim Crow" still dictated the course of American race relations, whether as law in the southern states where slavery had once prevailed or as extralegal practice in the rest of the country. Since the end of the nineteenth century, baseball had been part of an overall American pattern of racial discrimination and exclusion.

Relatively prosperous in the previous decade, black baseball in organized league form briefly disappeared altogether in the early Depression years. Although the economic crisis hit African Americans even harder than it did most whites, a new group of black baseball capitalists, often men closely tied to the urban black underworld, financed the creation of a new Negro National League in 1933 and, four years later, a Negro American League. More than ever, baseball was a vital element in the lives of African Americans, especially for the vast number of twentieth-century emigrants from the southern states who had settled in the swelling black districts of northern cities.

The Talent Pool, Then and Now

It seems a plausible conjecture that the professional baseball of the 1930s, while still played on opposite sides of the color line, featured more good players and more good play than at any time before or since in the sport's long history. Today's conventional wisdom holds that with a doubled national population, the breakdown of racial barriers, and the entry into the sport of steadily rising numbers of non-U.S. citizens, especially from Central America and the Caribbean, baseball's talent pool has become much bigger than it was sixty or seventy years ago. Later generations of athletes have also benefited from better diet, sophisticated physical conditioning regimes, and remarkable advances in the treatment of injuries and illnesses. . . .

Is today's baseball talent pool actually that much bigger than was the case in the 1930s? That's questionable. One should keep in mind the immense baseball universe that used to exist outside Organized Baseball. Once upon a time, baseball was king, for both spectators and participants. (Even if in the thirties nighttime recreational softball, playable under minimal outdoor lighting, was rapidly gaining in popularity among both men and women.) Baseball was still the game American children played everywhere (usually without today's omnipresent adult supervision), and millions of adult men continued to play—often into middle age—in organized "semipro" leagues in cities or in loosely structured competition between small towns and rural communities. So not only relatively but in absolute numbers more Americans were probably playing baseball in the 1930s than at any time since. . . .

Pay Cuts for Players

After reaching an average salary of about $7,500 in the previous decade, with a very few men such as Babe Ruth, Rogers Hornsby, and Ty Cobb drawing a great deal more, major leaguers saw their pay slashed by an average of about 25 percent during the lean early Depression years. The limited economic recovery that began in 1934 made for modest gains, although salary levels never returned to pre-Depression levels until the post–World War II years.

Yet even with the cuts they had to take, big-league ballplayers were still paid much better than wage earners in the general population—as had always been the case. A player earning only $3,000 in, say, 1932 was still making more than twice as much as the typical industrial worker (if that worker had somehow managed to hold on to a job), and at $3,000 one paid federal income taxes at the rate of about 1 percent annually. (By 1936 the rate had increased to 4 percent on a $6,000 income.) And if a particular ballplayer saw his salary reduced by 25 percent, he might take some comfort from the fact that from 1930 to 1933 wages nationally fell by more than half.

Rarely could a player gain a sympathetic hearing for his salary complaints in the baseball press. Sportswriters, usually getting by on skimpy pay themselves, had always tended to take the owners' side in salary disputes, and they were more than ever so disposed in the Depression years. The judgment of Ralph Davis, writing in 1934 out of Pittsburgh (where unemployment was particularly severe), was typical: "A ball player in the majors these days—when men in other professions are laboring for a mere pittance—if they are working at all—is mighty well paid for what he does . . . and he should stretch a mite to give service for what he receives." That same year, when Babe Ruth had to settle for $35,000 (after being cut from $80,000 in 1931 to $75,000 in 1932 and $52,000 in 1933), *Baseball Magazine* editorialized that "Babe now knows what millions of others have found out, how it seems to take a fifty per cent cut.". . . .

Although . . . Babe Ruth's unprecedented $80,000 per year salary for the 1930 and 1931 seasons [was] publicized and sportswriters continually made educated guesses about what other players were paid, both club owners and players usually considered final contract provisions as confidential matters between themselves and nobody else. As Charley Gehringer, Detroit's stellar second baseman, expressed it, "In those days, you didn't know what anybody made and didn't really seem to care."

If players had to take pay cuts from salaries that in most cases were hardly opulent to begin with, then they also played a kind of baseball that they and others who watched it would always insist was hungrier, rougher, and less forgiving than it became in later decades. For one thing, Depression-era men were more likely, in the argot of the game, to "play hurt." Gaining a place on a twenty-five-man big-league roster put one in an elite company of only four hundred such athletes in the world. Then, beginning with the 1932 season, club owners trimmed their rosters by two, thus sparing themselves the expense of thirty-two players' salaries.

The typical ballplayer of the 1930s, finding circumstances within his profession increasingly precarious (especially with many minor leagues folding), wasn't likely to let a nagging or even a bad injury keep him out of the lineup. In the first week of September 1934, as the Detroit Tigers drove for the American League pennant, shortstop Billy Rogell broke his ankle. He had it wrapped tightly and thickly and continued to play through the World Series. "Hell," said Rogell, "in those days you didn't want to get out of the lineup. Someone might take your job.". . . .

In the circumstances of the thirties, few ballplayers had much in the way of options for making a living outside baseball. Cleveland pitcher Mel Harder, who won 223 games over a twenty-year career in the majors, knew how much better off he was than most. "People were begging and out of work," he recalled. "I'd go back to Omaha, some of my best friends were pushing a rake or a shovel for the WPA [Works Progress Administration], making a dollar a day. And glad to get it."

A Rougher Game

The game on the field was rougher—at least it seems that way when one reads the frequent press accounts of basemen badly spiked by hard-sliding runners, of batters (in a time before batting helmets or forearm guards) hit by pitches and sometimes hospitalized, of genuine fistfights between players, players and managers, and occasionally even players and umpires. . . .

Baseball in the 1930s may not have been as chronically rowdy as that in the 1890s, but much of what happened in the Depression decade makes today's game appear downright genteel. For example, while batters have never liked it when pitchers throw "high and tight," in the thirties few questioned the prerogative of the man on the mound to keep the batter from crowding the plate. Nobody was supposed deliberately to throw at an opponent's head; pitchers suspected of intentional "beanings" or "skullings" were roundly condemned in the baseball press. But sixty or seventy years ago, batters simply expected to be knocked down and were prepared to duck. . . .

The Best Way to Earn a Living

The baseball of the Depression era paid less, left players essentially at the mercy of club owners, and probably demanded more in the way of physical endurance and tolerance of pain. Yet what comes through again and again in the reminiscences of the men who played back then is their deep and abiding love of the game itself— and their understanding of how truly fortunate they were. Lloyd Waner, who with his older brother, Paul, lined thousands of base hits for the Pittsburgh Pirates, later observed that the routine of ballplayers had them going from hotel to ballpark, back to the hotel, and then onto a train for another city, and that consequently they saw relatively little of the hardships most people were enduring. But at season's end, "my brother Paul and me would go back to Oklahoma, and then we would realize how bad things were. The farms were abandoned, the owners off to Lord knew where. Stores that had been doing business in the spring were boarded up. People were glum and poor. That was the real world."

For young men who possessed exceptional athletic skills but had little else going for them, baseball was more than ever the way to make a decent and perhaps handsome living. In 1937, his first full season in the majors, Elbie Fletcher was paid $3,700, but "I couldn't *believe* you could make that much money having fun." "Listen," said Leon "Goose" Goslin, an eighteen-year American League outfielder and Hall of Famer, "the truth is it was *more* than fun. It was heaven." And Bill Werber remembered one day, before a game at Fenway Park in Boston, sitting between Lefty Grove and catcher Rick Ferrell, both future Hall of Famers. "Can you imagine," mused Ferrell, "gettin' paid for doin' this?"

On the other side of the color line, excluded from Organized Baseball, black professional players had even fewer Depression-era options than whites. And just about everything—from roster sizes, league schedules, and press coverage to the crowds they were able to attract and the money they could make—was smaller still for them. One critical difference between their situation and that of their white counterparts was that while most black players signed contracts to play for a particular team in a particular season, there was no such thing as the reserve clause in black baseball. So baseball for African Americans suffered not only from a shaky financial structure but from chronically high turnover in player personnel—from season to season and even from month to month. Basically at liberty to play for whoever paid the most money, black players commonly became baseball vagabonds, moving from team to team in the United States and migrating to Cuba, Puerto Rico, Venezuela, Mexico, and the Dominican Republic for short-term and sometimes extended employment.

Woody Guthrie:
Songs for the People

Joe Klein

The years of the Great Depression were rich as far as music was concerned. Numerous different musical styles came of age during the 1930s. Bing Crosby crooned "Brother, Can You Spare a Dime?" while Billie Holiday was a major presence in the jazz scene with songs such as "Strange Fruit," her 1939 protest against the continued lynching of African Americans. But the genre of music perhaps most associated with the Depression was hillbilly, or folk music, which eventually evolved into country and western.

Woody Guthrie is one of the best-known folksingers to come out of this time. Guthrie is now best known for the songs he wrote about the plight of migrant workers during the Depression and for other political songs, including "This Land Is Your Land." His first big break, however, was as a radio show host in California. The following snippet from a Guthrie biography, *Woody Guthrie: A Life* by Joe Klein, describes the folksinger's adventures on his journey out west and how they influenced his music. Klein is the author of *Primary Colors* and is a Washington correspondent with the *New Yorker.*

[1936] was a strange moment in the Great Depression. The worst was supposed to be over, the economy was supposed to be improving . . . and life probably *was* better for some people. But for the rest—for those left hungry and jobless in a time of mild optimism—it seemed worse than ever. That certainly was true in the Southwest, where the dust and drought were only the most obvious signs of a general collapse. Even in fertile areas, small farmers were being driven out to make room for massive corporate entities that farmed with machines and could actually wring a profit from the land. The family farm simply wasn't economical anymore. A human convulsion of epic proportions was in progress. The whole countryside seemed to heave and groan as the farms emptied and the highways filled.

With all the homeless men cluttering the roadsides, Woody [Guthrie] was finding it difficult to hitch rides, and often had no choice but to travel by freight train. It still wasn't the most pleasant way for him to go, but, with his guitar slung over his shoulder, he was a popular figure in the boxcars and hobo jungles [the camps where hobos, or tramps, lived]. Inevitably, someone would ask him to play "Jesse James" or "Columbus Stockade" or "The Boll Weevil Song" or some other tune that a grandmother or uncle had sung back in the days when the family still had the farm; if he didn't know the words, they'd be more than happy to teach him. He was developing a repertoire of songs from all over the country—ballads from the Appalachians and Ozarks, cowboy songs, hoedowns and breakdowns, hymns and country blues from the black belt. Often, when he'd forget a verse, he'd make up another on the spot to replace it. The songs were always changing, reinventing themselves. With some, like "Lonesome Valley," it was hard to say where the traditional version left off and Woody's began.

Singing for the People

He played a variety of four- and six-stringed instruments, but none of them well. His guitar picking would never be much more than adequate. His singing voice was dry, flat, and hard like the country. It wasn't a very good voice, but it commanded attention: listening to him sing was bitter but exhilarating, like biting into a lemon. In any case, his level of musical virtuosity never mattered very much to his audiences on the road.

They always wanted to hear the old tunes—there weren't many requests for fox-trots in the boxcars—and Woody was amazed by the impact the songs had. Sometimes grown men would get all misty-eyed when he sang them, and their voices would catch when they tried to sing along. The whiney old ballads his mother had taught him were a bond that all country people shared; and now, for the migrants, the songs were all that was left of the land. . . . It wasn't just entertainment; he was performing their past. They listened closely, almost reverently, to the words. In turn, he listened to their life stories, and felt their pain and anger. An odd thought began to percolate. *He* was one of *them*. The collapse of his family wasn't all that unique; these people had seen hard times too. Almost every one of them had a story that was, if not as gruesome as his, bad enough. . . . Woody had never considered himself part of any group before. But here he was, an Okie, and these were his people.

Learning to Survive on the Road

He began to move in wider circles away from [his home in] Pampa [Texas] and during the next year was spotted everywhere from Ohio to California. He spent nights in jail on vagrancy charges when he was happy for the roof over his head; he spent nights in skid row flophouses that reeked of vomit and crawled with bedbugs; he spent nights out in the desert, freezing; he spent nights in the boxcars dodging randy old hoboes looking for boys to sleep with ("The Big Rock Candy Mountain," he learned, was a song about a homosexual tramp who seduces a young boy away from home); he learned to sleep on floors, in corners, on sidewalks, in alleys, anywhere. He was still learning, and quiet, and not yet ready to show very much of himself to the world . . . although he could, when necessary, stroll into a diner and start up a conversation with the orneriest waitress, spinning out tall tales about life on the road and serenading the customers with old favorites, and inevitably get someone—often the waitress herself—to pay for his bowl of chili. . . .

He always returned home to [his wife] Mary sooner or later, usually bedraggled and without any explanations. . . . Then he'd grow restless again. . . . Sometimes he'd tell her where he'd be going and when he'd be back, other times he'd leave a note on the refrigerator door, but often he'd just be gone.

The First Trip to California

He went to California. . . . It was an awful trip. The Los Angeles police, alarmed by the influx of migrants from the Southwest, had set up highly illegal roadblocks on the major highways at the California border, turning back people who looked like they might be "unemployables." Security on the railroads also was tightened—they called it the "Bum Blockade"—and Woody had to be careful not to get caught in the Glendale switching yards as he waited for a freight train. . . .

He spent several weeks with [his] Aunt Laura in Turlock, marveling at the size of the valley and its abundant harvest, the orchards stretching out forever in perfect lines of trees heavy with fruit. . . .

There was an anger in California, a bitterness toward his people—toward *him*—that Woody had never experienced before. It was frightening; he was stunned by the bigotry everywhere he went. In Los Angeles—a city where only 20 percent of the residents were natives—it was the nervous, priggish anger that recent immigrants often summon up to solidify their social standing in a new town. In the valley, it was the vicious, institutionalized violence of the vigilantes and hired goons who kept the migrants moving, meek and terrified.

The word "Okie" had become a slur, a word the goons spat out to describe *all* the migrants, all poor white people. About 500,000 "Okies" had entered the state since the beginning of the Depression, and there was widespread fear that California was being overrun. . . .

Inspired by the Wobblies

And now Woody began to listen more closely to the old radicals—all of whom seemed to be named Mac—who sat whispering around the campfires in the hobo jungles. They'd seen it all before. They had explanations. There were two sides, the rich and the poor, and you had to make your choice. They talked quickly, softly, insistently, hand on your elbow, about the workers organizing, facing down the bosses: it was possible; they had seen it. Some of them had been beaten and manhandled so many times their brains were soggy. They muttered half coherently about the capitalists, the rich bastards . . . and then, at the slightest encouragement, would reach into their pockets and pull out a battered old red card that proved they had been members of the wildest, woolliest, most violent, joyous, and completely disorganized gang of Reds ever to strike fear in the hearts of the American bourgeoisie: the International Workers of the World, or I.W.W., or more familiarly, the Wobblies. For a brief time before World War I, they had terrorized half the country and tried to organize the other half into One Big Union. They stood as a militant reproach to the moderate, cautious American Federation of Labor (A.F. of L.) and the increasingly tame Socialist Party. They led violent, futile strikes and advocated sabotage as a weapon in the class struggle a little too openly to be serious about it. If Samuel Gompers of the A.F. of L. said that his goal for the workers was, simply, "More," the Wobblies wanted more than that: "Bread and Roses Too" was the slogan of their 1912 textile strike in Lawrence, Massachusetts. Their brazen, arms-and-elbows style of radicalism was especially popular with the lumberjacks, the miners, and the migrant workers out West. It fit perfectly into the self-conscious romanticism of the hobo culture. The blunt, overstated Wobbly style was summed up beautifully in the I.W.W. *Preamble*, a simple one-page document which began: "The working class and the employing class have nothing in common. There can be no peace as long as hunger and want are found among millions of working people and the few, who make up the employing class, have all the good things in life."

In 1906, the Wobblies in Spokane had realized their street speakers were being drowned out by the noisy Salvation Army brass band. Ever resourceful, they decided to form their own band to mock the Salvation Army. Mac McLintock (who later said he wrote "Hallelujah I'm a Bum") and Jack Walsh wrote several parodies of Salvation Army hymns that were so successful the Wobblies put them out in a *Little Red Songbook*. . . .

Woody discovered the Wobblies just as he was getting angry about the horrors and deprivations all around him on the road. The *Red Songbook* parodies, with their inspired use of humor and music to convey anger, obviously had an impact. He began to write some parodies of his own, songs about things he'd seen like the Los Angeles police barricade at the California line—only he put his words to the old country tunes the Okies loved, instead of the popular melodies the Wobblies had used. His new songs were more serious and direct than [his earlier ones] but, at the same time, they were simpler and funnier. Woody was beginning to discover his remarkable ability to transform his anger into humor. . . .

In "Talking Dust Bowl," which he wrote and rewrote endlessly while riding the freights in 1936 and 1937, he re-created the migrant experience in six bitter, exquisitely simple verses. The song begins in 1927, a small but happy farmer hauling his crops into town, but then:

> Rain quit and the wind got high
> And a black old dust storm filled the sky
> And I swapped my farm for a Ford machine
> And I poured it full of this gasoline
> And I started. Rockin and a-rollin. Over the mountains,
>   out toward the old peach bowl.

The car has all sorts of trouble in the mountains, breaking down and falling apart. He has to push it uphill and tries to coast it downhill, but there's a hairpin turn and "I . . . didn't make it.". . . Finally, in the last verse, the family reaches the promised land:

> We got out to the west coast broke
> So dad gum hungry I thought I'd croak
> And I bummed up a spud or two
> And my wife fixed up a tater stew.
> We poured the kids full of it. Mighty thin stew, though;
>   you could read a magazine right through it.

Then, a *second* tag line:

> Always have figured that if it had been just a little bit thinner,
>   some of these here politicians could have seen through it.

When Woody said that word, "politicians," he rolled it over in his mouth, luxuriated in it, pulled and tugged at it in such a way—*pollli-TISH-uns*—that he was able to convey more rage and frustration than a dozen radical pamphlets. . . .

The Singing Cowboy

An amazing number of Guthries and assorted relatives congregated in the demure San Fernando Valley town of Glendale, just as they had converged on the Texas panhandle ten years earlier. Woody moved in with his Aunt Laura, who had tired of living up in Turlock, and he began hanging around with a cousin, Jack Guthrie. . . .

Jack was about Woody's age. He was tall, handsome in a boyish, western sort of way, and very talented. He had a beautiful, smooth tenor voice [and] played the guitar much better than Woody. . . .

It was the heyday of the singing cowboy in Los Angeles, a

strange and rather wacky era that was mostly the result of Hollywood's desire to combine two of its most popular forms, the Western and the musical. . . . The music itself didn't bear the vaguest resemblance to the real cowboy ballads that Woody knew, like "Sam Bass" or "Buffalo Skinners." With all the yodeling and barbershop quartet harmony, it sounded more like Switzerland than Texas. But it was one of the biggest things in Los Angeles, and you couldn't turn on a radio without hearing the Sons of the Pioneers (whose lead singer, Leonard Slye, would become Roy Rogers) or some other group crooning a love song to their cattle.

Jack Guthrie, whose nickname was "Oklahoma" or "Oke," was intent on becoming a singing cowboy star and invited Woody along as his sidekick. Woody was doubtful about the project, but it was a lot more interesting than washing dishes in Strangler Lewis's restaurant in Glendale, which is what he'd been doing until he tried to clean an aluminum pot with lye water and smoked out the place. . . .

Jack found work for them in a cowboy vaudeville show that performed for several days between screenings of "Waikiki Wedding" at the Strand Theater in Long Beach. Also on the bill were the famous country music group the Beverly Hillbillies, as well as Woody's distant cousins Possum Trot Bruce and the Poe Boys. Jack stole the show with his beautiful rendition of "Empty Bunk in the Cothouse Tonight," but Woody was far less prominent, coming on with the rodeo clowns and rattling his spoons. . . .

Buoyed by that success, Jack talked his way into a radio audition at KFVD, a station known more for its political commentary than its music. It was owned by a crusty old populist named J. Frank Burke, a small, florid man with white hair, whose major interest was his own "Editor of the Air" program each day at noon. Jack managed to convince Burke that the station needed a cowboy show to liven its programming and, on July 19, 1937, "The Oklahoma and Woody Show" made its debut at 8 A.M. on KFVD. They weren't paid anything for the privilege of appearing on the radio each day, but Jack didn't care: he saw the show as a promotional tool, a way to publicize personal appearances at rodeos, saloons, and other staples of the local cowboy circuit.

The show itself was mostly Jack, with only a smattering of

Woody. They would sing their theme song, "Lonesome Road Blues," and harmonize a few other songs together. Then Jack would take over, singing and yodeling in the Jimmie Rodgers fashion, with Woody backing him on the guitar and harmonica. Very rarely did Woody solo, usually a harmonica tune or some other novelty number. He didn't exactly enjoy this arrangement—cowboy music wasn't at all his style—but he *was* on the radio in Los Angeles and, what's more, the show was a success. They received more than three hundred fan letters in August and, by September, Burke had decided to put them on twice a day, adding another half hour at 11 P.M.

Early on, Jack had introduced Woody to his closest friends in California, the Crissman family. . . . The older daughter, Maxine, was a slim, elegant-looking woman with a husky voice who liked dressing up in high-fashion style. She worked in a dress factory for fourteen dollars per week, and hated it. . . .

Woody (who was obviously getting impatient with the same old cowboy stuff) asked Jack if he could invite Maxine on the show to sing a duet with him. Jack, always amenable, didn't mind at all. They sang "Curly-Headed Baby," and it went quite well. . . .

Here Come Woody and Lefty Lou

During the next few weeks, they made several public appearances and sounded great each time. Woody was very casual about it all: there were no rehearsals, no instructions, no planning, no worrying. He'd just step up to the microphone, say "Howdy" to the folks, start singing . . . and expect that she'd do the same. After appearing on the "Cowtown" radio program and at "Frontier Day" at Hermosa Beach, they returned to "The Oklahoma and Woody Show" on September 3, and Woody wrote a little introduction for Maxine. He called her "Lefty Lou from Ole Mizzoo . . . She's long-winded and left-handed, and she can jump a six-rail fence with a bucket of milk in each hand and never cause a ripple on the surface . . ."

Without any maneuvering or arranging on Woody's part, without any apparent effort at all—it was so maddeningly nonchalant—the breaks began to fall just right for them. In early September, Jack Guthrie realized he wasn't making enough money in show business to support his family, and decided to go back to construction work for a while. . . . Woody asked Maxine to join him on both the morning and evening shows. She happily quit her job in the dress factory, and Woody wrote a new theme song to the tune of "Curly-Headed Baby":

> Drop whatever you are doing
> Stop your work and worry too;
> Sit right down and take it easy
> Here come Woody and Lefty Lou

. . . There were no scripts, no song lists; in between numbers they'd chat amiably about what to sing next, or read a letter from a listener requesting a certain song. At least once a show, Woody would spin off a tall tale, or a thought for the day. He called it his "Cornpone Philosophy," and played at sounding like an utter yokel, a device that enabled him to get off some good licks not only at the city slickers but also at the narrow-mindedness and insularity of country folk.

The warm, homespun style of the show found a natural audience in Los Angeles. The city was filled with people who missed their old lives on the farm, who found urban life just a bit too fast, who busily organized themselves into home-state societies—clubs for natives of Iowa, Oklahoma, and so forth—that held regular meetings in the downtown cafeterias and massive annual picnics. They were an older, emotional, and unpretentious audience, who quickly adopted Woody and Lefty Lou as members of the family. And it wasn't just in Los Angeles: the 11 P.M. show skipped out across the country (often, on a good night, it could be heard clearly in Pampa), and there seemed to be people all over who were nostalgic for the sweet, simple country life. . . .

On November 12, 1937, Woody and Maxine signed a one-year contract with Standard Broadcasting Company. After receiving their first paycheck, Woody dragged her over to the bank at the Ambassador Hotel and had it cashed into silver dollars, big clunky pieces of metal they could stack and play with—ten for Maxine and ten for Woody. [It was his first paycheck as an entertainer.]

The Controversial Comedy of *Amos 'n' Andy*

Elizabeth McLeod

Radio became a significant means of mass communication during the Depression years. Over the airwaves, President Franklin Roosevelt was able to speak directly to the American people during weekly broadcasts called Fireside Chats. Radio was also the central form of at-home entertainment during these years—it was the television of its day. People listened to baseball games, and families sat around their radios enjoying the comedy of George Burns and Gracie Allen on their program, *George and Gracie*. Poverty and the hard times of the day were topics of *Little Orphan Annie*, a radio show based on the comic strip.

One controversial radio program was called *Amos 'n' Andy*. Freeman Gosden and Charles Correll wrote and starred in this situation comedy about two African American men, Amos and Andy. Gosden and Correll were white and were seen by many as racists who did nothing but further stereotypes about African Americans by continuing the tradition of minstrel shows. In a minstrel show, white men blackened their faces and performed parodies of African Americans. There were those who saw something more in *Amos 'n' Andy*, however. The following excerpt from broadcast historian Elizabeth McLeod's "Amos 'n' Andy in Person: The Origins of a Radio Landmark," describes the African American response to the program in the early 1930s.

> *They do not belittle the Negro and I think their programs have done more to help the white people understand us than all the books ever written.*
> —Rooming House Owner, Harlem, 1930

There is a positive disapproval of the exploitation of two types of Negro for the sole purpose of making money at the expense of a group of people who need every helpful influence it can get from every source possible.
—Editorial, Pittsburgh *Courier*, 1931

Even in an era in which less than eight per cent of African-American families owned radios, there was no consensus among black listeners over the meaning of "Amos 'n' Andy." Nor did this debate begin entirely out of the earshot of the white press. In the spring of 1930, as part of its detailed exploration of the various facets of the "Amos 'n' Andy" phenomenon, *Radio Digest* sent correspondent A.W. Clarke to Harlem and to the black district of Hartford, Connecticut, to interview a cross-section of black residents about their feelings regarding the program, and the results were published in the magazine's August 1930 issue. Some responses were positive, with praise ranging from guarded to enthusiastic—

It is the height of art for any man to give the public such clean entertainment nightly, even though the thoughts of one night do not always connect with those of another. With certain types of colored people even in our day, the Amos and Andy stuff is natural, though as a whole we are growing away from it. The younger generation naturally considers itself above that and cannot appreciate it. Yet Amos and Andy are harming no one.
—Dr. F.A. Hinkinson, dentist, 1335 Main Street, Hartford

When I first heard Amos and Andy, I thought they were Negroes, and while their composition did not appeal to the esthetic, their humor being true, was great. Then I thought, here are two colored men giving a showing equally with other artists to demonstrate their genius. They are not elevating nor degrading the race, but since what they do has a national appeal and has captured the public fancy, hurrah for them! I was surprised when I learned they were white. My opinion of them has not changed.
—Rev. R. A. Moody, Baptist minister, 556 Martin Street, Hartford

There is something charming about Amos 'n' Andy that holds any person's attention. If they were attacking the colored people, their entertainment would have died long ago, but what they are saying is so humorous and free from the taint of prejudice I do not see how any person, white or colored can take it in a personal way. . . . The reason why I believe no modern colored comedian could surpass them is this. The modern Negro is too self-conscious. To give you an example of what I mean, I have a friend who owns a radio. He never misses Amos 'n' Andy when home among his family, but when in the presence of white people he just cannot stand to listen

to them. I will listen to Amos 'n' Andy in any place among any crowd. Amos 'n' Andy have this race down pat, I am telling you.
　　　　　　　—Name withheld, barbershop patron, Hartford

. . . But other responses gathered by the *Radio Digest* correspondent revealed a range of criticisms, ranging from mild annoyance to outright anger over the images portrayed in the program.

If you want my personal opinion, here it is—Amos and Andy are commercializing certain types of Negro characters, as they could not find anything among the whites to amuse the general public.
　　　　　　　—Name withheld, barbershop proprietor, Hartford

No real Negro wants to burlesque his people the way they are doing in this enlightened age. . . . Let two Negroes do those same things—that is, speak and act like Amos and Andy—and they would not be long at it, for not only would their own race would not listen to them, but would wage constant war against them. . . .
　　　　　　　—M.A. Johnson, undertaker, 19 Pavillion Street, Hartford

Only the most illiterate type of Negro will speak as Amos and Andy do, and that type is fast leaving us.
　　　　　　　—Name withheld, attorney, Hartford

Amos and Andy do not appeal to me. If they were Negroes it would be the same. If I were white it would make no difference.
　　　　　　　—Rev. W.O. Carrington, Methodist minister,
　　　　　　　　　　　　　2084 Main Street, Hartford

If they were Negroes, I should think that they were making fools of the race.
—F.L. Peterson, professor of English, 134 Camden Street, Boston

Debate in the Black Press

The *Radio Digest* article offered the first hint of controversy brewing around the program to appear in a mainstream publication—but the debate would take on greater signficance during 1930–31 in the pages of the African-American press. As far back as 1928, Correll and Gosden had been praised by the Chicago *Defender,* then the nation's leading black newspaper—and had received additional favorable coverage from that publication in the years since. Their program had also received positive attention in the pages of several other African-American papers during 1930, including the Baltimore *Afro-American,* the Philadelphia *Tribune,* and the Kansas City *Call.* But in December 1930, W.J. Walls, Chicago bishop of the African Methodist Episcopal Zion Church, and one of the nation's best-known black churchmen, sharply denounced "Amos 'n' Andy" in an article published in *Abbott's Monthly* magazine—a cultural and literary journal founded and owned by Chicago *Defender* publisher Robert Abbott. Walls was already noted as a crusader against jazz and other types of popular entertainment, music, and literature that he believed exploited the "primitive weakness" of the lower classes in black America— which he dismissed as "the unlettered and mentally imbecilic group of our race"—and he used his article on "Amos 'n' Andy" as a platform to second scholar and social historian Benjamin Brawley's overall denunciations of the "sordidness, realism, vulgarity, psychoanalysis, free verse, and staccato writing" which he felt characterized much of the literature by and about black Americans. Like Brawley, Walls had no use for any form of ghetto imagery in depictions of black America by black authors—and even less tolerance of such images when they came from white authors like Correll and Gosden. Walls' criticism of "Amos 'n' Andy" took particular aim at the lower-class characterizations, contending that they failed to show any evidence of "the highest intuitions of the civilized man," and that the "crude, repetitional, and moronic" dialogue of the program had a "somnolent effect upon the minds of many of our people, especially of the youth."

The Campaign Against "Amos 'n' Andy"

Four months later, Walls' theme was picked up by Robert Vann, publisher of the Pittsburgh *Courier,* then the nation's second-largest black newspaper. In the spring of 1931, Vann and his chief editorial writer George S. Schuyler—a combative, hyperbolic journalist . . . who shared Benjamin Brawley's contempt for representations of ghetto life—proclaimed the start of a nationwide campaign to drive "Amos 'n' Andy" from the air.

> *The characters portray two types of Negro to be found in the United States. The men portraying the characters are white. The company employing Amos 'n' Andy is white. The people reaping the financial gain from the characterizations are all white.*
>
> *But the people who are getting the black eye out of it all are the Negroes*

*of this country, and of every other country where Negroes are found. . . .
There is a positive disapproval of the exploitation of two types of Negro for
the sole purpose of making money at the expense of a group of people who
need every helpful influence it can get from every source possible.*

*And what is the damage done? Who can appraise it? What is the im-
pression made? It is almost everywhere to be met where white people en-
counter Negroes. It is now a common thing for salesmen to enter a Negro
business place and begin by asking 'Did you hear "Amos 'n' Andy" last
night?' This is the 'opening' used as the method of approach. On the
streets, in the banks, in the business places, Negro help is often referred to
as Amos or Andy. Negroes are being put down as being one of two types.
We are either Amos or we are Andy.*

*If we can continue the fight as started, we may be able to persuade ex-
ploiters that we are not such fools as to spend our money to see ourselves
classified below our own ideals. The fight is on.*

—Editorial, Pittsburgh *Courier*, 4/25/31

While there is no questioning Vann's commitment to the cause
of black advancement, he was also a businessman—and by the
time of the "Amos 'n' Andy" campaign, the publisher had ac-
quired something of a reputation as an opportunist, with a history of mounting elaborate crusades and then dropping them just
as abruptly when they failed to sufficiently spur the circulation
of his paper. . . .

The crusade against "Amos 'n' Andy" became a focus of
circulation-building efforts for the *Courier* during 1931. Whatever
Vann's exact motives were in mounting the campaign, the pages
of the *Courier* were filled for nearly six months with anti–"Amos
'n' Andy" articles, editorials, and letters from readers. Petition
forms were published, and readers were encouraged to circulate
them, toward a final goal of one million signatures, with the
progress of the drive tracked by a weekly front-page graphic. . . .

As the campaign advanced [through] the summer of 1931 and
activist readers gave the petition forms wide circulation, the
Courier promised its readers that a team of lawyers were preparing to file for an injunction in Cook County Superior Court in
Chicago that would halt the broadcast of "Amos 'n' Andy," and
that five thousand clergymen would preach sermons against the
program on a given Sunday in October. However, none of these
goals were met. No court action was ever filed. Although a num-

ber of ministers nationwide did preach sermons urging black Americans to develop self-respect on the Sunday designated, few appear to have mentioned "Amos 'n' Andy." And far from gathering universal support, the campaign was publicly repudiated by a broad cross-section of other black papers. . . .

No Universal Support in the Black Media

Another black paper, the Louisville *News*, rejected the *Courier*'s call to action by declaring that it was "utterly unable to work up a sweat over 'Amos 'n' Andy'"—

> *For every two Negroes that talk like 'Amos 'n' Andy' there are twenty thousand Colored Americans far removed from them in intelligence, in speech and in character. Our white neighbors know this as well as we know it, and the race is not affected.*
> —Editorial, Louisville *News*, reprinted in Kansas City *Call*, 8/28/31

Over a three-issue span in the fall of 1931, Seattle's African-American paper, the *Northwest Enterprise* published a lengthy rebuttal to the *Courier*'s denunciation of "Amos 'n' Andy," arguing that Correll and Gosden were merely reflecting everyday reality in their portrayal of Amos, Andy, and their friends, dismissing the protest as "rather far-fetched," and sharply criticizing those who presumed to speak for the entire race in condemning the program.

> *This newspaper is a champion of the self-respect doctrine for worthy Negroes as individuals or as a race group. It has been fighting for many years for just that thing. Our contention is that despite warnings of many years, the Negroes who have elected to call themselves leaders and shapers of the destiny of the race are conducting a very fine burlesque on the "Fresh Air Taxicab" business. If Negro newspapers and self-elected Negro leaders would inaugurate and keep going every day in the week a campaign to teach Negroes self-respect, it would be more impressive and do more good than picking out some comedy skit which reveals so much truth until it hurts those who inwardly acknowledge how very true it really is. . . .*

> *Go into any Negro business concern or quarter, and there you will find characters in real Negro life who do not measure up to the qualifications of Amos, who use the worst language imaginable, and whose judgement is below zero. They are unreliable, and have simply a get-by policy. If two-thirds of the Negroes who run two-by-four business excuses had as capable owners as Amos, the race would be better represented. To say that Amos is a burlesque is to put the cart before the horse. . . .*

> *The Negro race has types like Mr. Andrew [Andy] Brown by the car-*

loads—Negroes who try to ape everybody and everything that looks big—ignorant Negroes who enter in where real worthy people would fear to tread. There are Negroes in business and in church who will promise anything when they know they have no way on earth to keep the promise. This runs true for the Negro preacher down to the Negro hot-dog seller. All this class wants is a scheme to get by, and they only get by because more worthy and misled Negroes help them by. Their pictures are ever in the paper. They thrive on publicity and spend their time and money 'dolling up' in 'fronts' for public praise, hoping to appear as prosperous business assets.

Let Negro pulpit and press center on these Andys in real life, and they need not worry about Andy on the air.

       —"The Campaign Against 'Amos 'n' Andy,'"
          Northwest Enterprise, 11/5/31

And from Harlem's *Amsterdam News,* Vann's campaign drew only a cutting rebuke—

The Courier *campaign will serve one good end. When they complete their tally of signatures, we will know precisely how many halfwits there are in the race.*

       —Theophilus Lewis, *Amsterdam News,* 7/22/31

Unable to rally a majority of the black press in support of its cause, by late summer, the *Courier* was attempting to frame the protest along lines of social class and intelligence—and the paper's editorials took on a tone of desperation, denouncing black supporters of "Amos 'n' Andy" as harshly as they attacked the program itself.

Our protest has the sanction of all intelligent people, white and black. We do not expect ignorant Negroes and whites to be able to see the insult. We are not looking for the 'Amos 'n' Andy' Negro to join our protest. We are happy to have the intelligence of both races indorsing our program. It has grown beyond the proportions of a joke; it has reached the serious stage. We are going on—with the help of all, if possible, but without the help of the ignorant, if we must.

      —"The 'Amos 'n' Andy' Tag," Pittsburgh *Courier,* 8/29/31

The *Courier's* Campaign Against the Show Ends

Six months after it began, the *Courier* without explanation abandoned the campaign. "We finally had to give it up," recalled

Jessie Vann, Robert Vann's widow, "because seemingly we were not accomplishing anything, unless it was popularizing [the program], for the radio program continued to have just as many listeners as before, and among our own people." No verified, independent count of petition signatures was ever made, but the paper claimed in October 1931 to have gathered 675,000 names in opposition to "Amos 'n' Andy." Despite Vann's published claims, the national office of the NAACP [National Association for the Advancement of Colored People] never endorsed the *Courier*'s drive, nor was there any consensus among local chapters: while an official of the Memphis, Tennessee, chapter of the organization proclaimed his support for the campaign, the president of the Casper, Wyoming, chapter denounced the effort as a publicity stunt for the newspaper—and endorsed "Amos 'n' Andy" as "good humorous entertainment."

The End of Prohibition

Carl H. Miller

On January 16, 1920, the Eighteenth Amendment became law, effectively banning the production, sale, and distribution of alcoholic beverages in the United States and beginning the period in history known as Prohibition. Following ratification of the amendment, the Volstead Act defined alcoholic beverages as containing more than .5 percent alcohol per volume.

There had always been organizations and individuals strongly for and against Prohibition, but by the 1930s more and more people were protesting the law. For one thing, many gangs ran speakeasies—illegal bars—and owned breweries that illegally brewed alcoholic beer. The struggle among gangs for a monopoly on the production and selling of beer led to violent battles called "beer wars." The start of the Great Depression also helped change the thinking of even fervent supporters of Prohibition, because the government could earn a lot of money from taxing beer were it made legal again. The following article by Carl H. Miller describes the end of Prohibition in the United States. Miller is a beer historian and the host of the American Brewery History Page at www.beerhistory.com.

On Saint Valentine's Day of 1929, love was decidedly not in the air on Chicago's north side. Six bodies lay dead and mutilated on the floor of a North Clark Street garage. A seventh victim had been rushed away barely clinging to life, only to succumb a short time later.

It was a scene probably more gruesome than any of the dozen or so lingering Chicago detectives had ever seen. The only remaining witness—a chained German shepherd—barked rabidly in one corner of the garage, and lunged at anyone who tried to quiet him. Outside, a thickening crowd of onlookers strained to catch a glimpse of the carnage, while a steady parade of city officials rolled up to the curb and marched inside to survey the aftermath. It was, after all, the worst episode yet in nearly a decade of Chicago's notoriously violent Prohibition-era beer wars.

Nevertheless, the seven unfortunate men who lost their lives on that day were a mere drop in the bucket. By the late 1920s, Chicago authorities were reporting between 350 and 400 gangland murders per year. Beer was big business, and mobsters stopped at nothing to gain and keep control of it. The infamous Al Capone (commonly blamed for the Saint Valentine's Day Massacre, though never charged) controlled no less than a half-dozen of Chicago's old breweries. Each was licensed to produce nonalcoholic near beer, but all churned out a steady flow of the real stuff. The *Chicago Tribune* estimated that, at its peak, the city's organized crime syndicates operated some 10,000 speakeasies, the proceeds from beer alone totaling $3.5 million per week.

And, of course, the Windy City [Chicago] was not alone in its bootlegger woes. Virtually every city in the nation was riddled with illegal trafficking in beer and whiskey, and the violence that it bred.

With each new report of sickening violence, public indignation toward the national dry law mounted. Though many felt little sorrow for the mostly mobster victims, the rampant political corruption that fueled the violence stirred anger in the hearts of most Americans. It seemed as though everyone from the cop on the beat right up to high-ranking federal officials was on the take.

Indeed, the stench of political corruption during the dry years did not stop even at the White House doors. President [Warren] Harding's attorney general, Harry Daugherty, was forced to resign amid allegations that he and his staff had accepted $250,000 from a wealthy Ohio bootlegger in exchange for immunity from prosecution. The very government that had foisted an unpopular law on the people was now exploiting the law for personal profit. It was exactly this sort of hypocrisy that enraged America and ignited a vigorous crusade to end the "Noble Experiment."

Turning the Tide

Even before national Prohibition took effect on January 16, 1920, efforts to repeal it were already under way in some circles. Among the most notable of the wet [anti-Prohibition] organizations was the Association Against the Prohibition Amendment (AAPA), formed in Washington, DC, in 1919. Its members were mainly big industry capitalists who feared that the loss of government revenue from beer taxes would bring both increased taxes for big corporations and a rise in personal income taxes for the wealthy. The AAPA made it a well-publicized edict that financial contributions from beer interests would never be allowed to exceed one-twentieth of its operating budget. In so doing, the association hoped to be somewhat free of the taint of blatant self-interest that had so plagued the brewers' efforts to quash Prohibition.

Backed by scores of millionaire industrialists, the AAPA found little difficulty in matching, or exceeding, the coffers of well-established Prohibition groups like the Anti-Saloon League and the Women's Christian Temperance Union. And like those organizations, the AAPA was masterful in its use of propaganda, particularly in wielding inflammatory statistics that tended to show the utter failure of the Eighteenth Amendment. In 1928, for example, the AAPA reported that, by its estimate, some 15 million pounds of hops had been sold during the year—enough to make 20 million barrels of illicit beer. The colossal loss to the government in beer taxes alone, argued the AAPA, was reason enough to end Prohibition.

Naturally, the nation's brewers agreed whole-heartedly with that logic. Prohibition had all but destroyed their industry. Most were finding great difficulty in surviving on the production of near beer while the steady flow of real beer from bootleggers went virtually unchallenged. August A. Busch, head of Anheuser-Busch in St. Louis, spoke for all brewers when he appealed to the American public in 1921: "Those who are obeying the law are being ground to pieces by its very operation, while those who are violating the law are reaping unheard-of rewards. Every rule of justice has been reversed." But, cries of economic injustice had not been successful for the brewers before Prohibition, and they were not terribly effective now. Likewise, the AAPA's message—often fraught with cold financial statistics and lofty economic theory—did not always find ready significance among the average working American.

Somewhat ironically, perhaps the most well-received grass roots initiative against Prohibition came from the wives of the AAPA's directors. In May of 1929, Pauline Sabin, wife of AAPA treasurer Charles Sabin, founded the Women's Organization for National Prohibition Reform (WONPR). The Sabin Women, as they were called, were headed largely by well-to-do wives of American industrialists. Their high social status brought frequent press coverage for their cause and gave a distinctly fashionable visage to the anti-Prohibition movement. For housewives throughout middle America, joining the WONPR was an otherwise inaccessible opportunity to mingle with high society. In less than two years, almost 1.5 million Sabin Women were sounding the depravity of bootlegger violence and political corruption.

Most Prohibitionists seethed over the escalating role that women were playing in the drive for repeal of the Eighteenth Amendment. After all, it had always been a sort of sacred presumption that the drys could count on the near unanimous support of women everywhere. Their defection now, even if in the minority, was a tough pill to swallow for hard-line Prohibitionists, who rarely missed an opportunity to exhibit their animosity over the issue. One dry advocate commented in the press, rather viciously, that, "these wet women, though rich most of them are, are no more than the scum of the earth, parading around in skirts, and possibly late at night flirting with other women's husbands at drunken and fashionable resorts."

Beer for Prosperity

When the Women's Organization for National Prohibition Reform first embarked on its campaign against the national dry law, the 1920s were still roaring loudly in America. Eliminating the violent crime and political corruption spread by bootleggers was the central goal of the organization. What the Sabin Women did not know was that, in just a matter of months, the whole rationale upon which the repeal movement was based would change abruptly and radically. On October 17, 1929, one of the most prosperous eras in American history came to a crashing halt. Black Tuesday had struck with unbelievable force, and the nation was plunged into economic depression. Suddenly, the crusade to repeal Prohibition took on an entirely new importance.

As unemployment reached epidemic proportions, few could deny the obvious truth that legalizing beer would create thousands of new jobs virtually over night. At the same time, desperately-needed new government revenue would be generated in the form of beer taxes. "Beer For Prosperity" became the anti-Prohibition battle cry. In New York City, Mayor Jimmy Walker demonstrated his support for the cause by organizing a day-long Beer Parade on May 14, 1932. An estimated 100,000 people turned out to cheer for the legalization of beer. One New Yorker in attendance, a toddler, held a sign that read, "My daddy had beer, why can't I?" Some 40,000 Detroiters held a similar event in the Motor City on the very same day. Marchers in the parade chanted "Who wants a bottle of beer?," baiting spectators to call back, "I do!"

Of course, the Depression notwithstanding, the dry forces were still everywhere in evidence. Both the Anti-Saloon League and the Women's Christian Temperance Union remained in full force, spewing propaganda and lobbing venomous rhetoric as aggressively as ever. Henry Ford, a famously vocal dry, announced that if Prohibition were repealed, he would abandon the automobile business: "I wouldn't be interested in putting automobiles into the hands of a generation soggy with drink." *The New Yorker* magazine took particular exception to Ford's ridiculous comment. Noting Detroit's unmatched reputation as a smuggling center for Canadian beer and whiskey, the magazine wrote, "It would be a great pity to have Detroit's two leading industries destroyed in one blow."

A Campaign Issue

Not surprisingly, Prohibition was a hot-button issue at the 1932 Democratic National Convention. In his speech, presidential nominee Franklin D. Roosevelt all but declared war on the dry law, pledging to "favor the modification of the Volstead Act just as fast as the Lord will let us to authorize the manufacture and sale of beer." It was, of course, the only stance he could take on the issue. Whether Democrat or Republican, wet or dry, voters understood that America was in economic crisis. Unemployment spoke louder than intemperance.

Indeed, Roosevelt's strong pro-repeal platform produced many political converts. Industrialist and staunch Republican Pierre Du Pont, for example, made news when he switched political parties solely on the basis of the repeal issue. Then, too, many former supporters of Prohibition itself had turned coat by this time. Ardent dry activist John D. Rockefeller Jr. stunned everyone when he announced in 1932 that he would no longer support Prohibition, calling it a "regrettable failure." Newspaper magnate William Randolph Hearst was another convert, and perhaps the most outspoken one. He put his nationwide chain of newspapers to work preaching the pros of repeal. After Roosevelt's landslide victory in November of 1932, Hearst's newspapers carried a celebratory article entitled "Beer By Christmas!"

Although Hearst's prediction was a bit premature, congressional action on the matter did, in fact, get under way even before the president-elect took office. In December, hearings were begun for the purpose of making severe changes to the Volstead Act. There was little question that the legalization of beer would be the ultimate outcome. There was disagreement, however, over what ought to be the maximum legal alcohol content of beer.

Brewers were brought in to testify on the issue. Among them was Boston brewery owner T.C. Haffenreffer, who pontificated, "all brews improve in taste, flavor and aroma directly in ratio with the increased alcoholic content." That, said Haffenreffer, was the "prime reason for desiring the maximum permissible alcoholic strength of our products." August A. Busch echoed that view, though his rationale was somewhat less tactful: "[People] want and are demanding a beer in all respects satisfying, and that will, so to say, furnish that warmth, satisfaction, and contentment that a mild stimulant like a good, wholesome beer supplies."

The debate lingered into 1933. Nine days after taking office on March 4, President Roosevelt sent a directive to Congress urging them to settle the matter. In the end, the figure of 3.2 percent alcohol by volume was agreed upon as the new allowable limit for beer under the Volstead Act. It wasn't the hearty 6 or 7 percent of pre-Prohibition days, but it was a victory, nonetheless. The Eighteenth Amendment, after all, remained in full effect, at least for the moment. Congress was simply exercising its right to modify the definition of an "intoxicating beverage." But for beer drinkers, it was a banner day. After 13 long years, beer was finally back, and Americans everywhere reveled in it.

Happy Days Are Here Again

At 12:01 A.M. on April 7, 1933, brewery whistles around the country heralded the return of beer. Throughout the night before (fondly dubbed "New Beer's Eve"), jubilant beer drinkers lined up outside breweries, anxious for their first taste of legal beer. In Milwaukee, where crowds were said to have been 50,000-strong at the breweries, beer drinkers hauled away their precious kegs and cases in everything from wheelbarrows to baby carriages. In New York City, movie houses played the newly-released film, "Beer Is Back!" Around the country, night clubs, hotels and restaurants—most filled beyond capacity—struggled to keep the taps flowing as raucous crowds downed an amazing 1.5 million barrels of beer during the first 24 hours that beer was back.

Many grateful brewery owners sent complimentary shipments of beer to President Roosevelt. August A. Busch made his presidential delivery in grand fashion, employing a bright red beer wagon drawn by six Clydesdale horses. The spectacle, of course, has since become a sacred corporate symbol for Anheuser-Busch. Officials at the Yuengling Brewery of Pottsville, PA, were dismayed to learn that their shipment of beer to Washington arrived missing 73 cases. Indeed, as truckloads of beer crossed America's highways during those first few days, some brewers were compelled to hire armed guards to protect their beer shipments against hijackers.

The Sobering Reality

Once all of the ballyhoo of New Beer's Eve and New Beer's Day had subsided, beer drinkers and brewers awoke to a sobering reality. The 5¢ mug of beer—a time-honored institution before Prohibition—was but a quaint memory now. For the better part of a half-century before Prohibition, the federal tax on beer was fixed at just $1 per barrel. Only during times of war was the tax increased temporarily. But those days were gone forever. Congress had re-legalized beer largely on the basis of its potential as a government revenue builder. Accordingly, the federal tax was set at $5 per barrel, plus a $1,000 annual license fee for each brewery. Today, the prevailing tax of $18 per barrel (though lower for production under 60,000 barrels) suggests that beer's role as an important federal revenue stream remains fully intact.

Heavy taxation of beer, however, is not Prohibition's only surviving legacy. A strong regulatory environment was also a key
component of repeal. First and foremost, lawmakers were eager
to legislate against the historically tight relationship between
brewers and saloons. The "tied house" system, according to its op-
ponents, gave rise to the "poor moral condition" of America's saloons and was the very fuel that drove the Prohibition movement.
Even today, there remains a strictly-regulated separation between
brewer and retailer. The old-time saloon itself, in fact, was a ca-
sualty of Prohibition. The designations "tavern," "club," "bar," and
"café" were much preferred by entrepreneurs hoping to side-step
the stigma of pre-Prohibition "grogshops" and Prohibition-era
speakeasies. Some state legislatures even sought to erase all rem-
nants of the old-fashioned saloon environment. Swinging doors,
for example, were outlawed in some regions. In others, the law
required that bar stools be provided for all patrons since it was
thought that standing at the bar—a venerable saloon tradition—
promoted excessive drinking.

Government regulation, however, did little to restrain what
was perhaps Prohibition's most sinister outgrowth. The criminal
groups which had made widespread disobedience possible—and
profitable—throughout Prohibition emerged in 1933 strong, well
financed and well connected. Crime was now organized, and
these criminal institutions are with us still today.

But, without question, the most critical legacy of America's
dry era is the wisdom offered by its monumental failure. The
Eighteenth Amendment was officially and forever repealed on
December 5, 1933, with the ratification of the Twenty-First
Amendment. To this day, national Prohibition remains the only
constitutional amendment ever to be repealed.

Communities
and Support

CHAPTER
4

Chapter Preface

When the Depression hit, few federal programs were in place to offer lasting relief for the people who suffered the greatest losses. Instead, people within disenfranchised communities banded together to help each other.

Farmers protested against banks that tried to take over fellow farmers' land. In Harlem, people paid to attend "rent parties" in order to help a neighbor pay the rent. Hoboes and tramps developed a code of ethics as well as a secret set of symbols they would etch in the dirt or draw on walls to signal whether a particular town or community was likely to help them or whether one should just keep moving.

This chapter looks at how some communities struggled and worked together through these hard years.

It's Not All Swing: Poverty and Hardship in Harlem

Ollie Stewart

During the 1920s and 1930s, African American art, literature, and dance flourished in what became known as the Harlem Renaissance. Jazz musicians such as Duke Ellington and singers such as Billie Holiday played in Harlem cabarets, and the exotic nightlife of this predominantly African American community was a major draw for well-to-do New Yorkers, black and white. This was only one side of Harlem, however. Residents of the New York City neighborhood suffered from extreme poverty, often living in substandard tenements at rents they struggled to afford. The following article by Ollie Stewart, staff writer for the *New York Times*, describes this bleaker side of Harlem during the Depression years. It appeared in the *New York Times* on October 1, 1939.

N orth of Central Park, from 110th Street to 155th, from Fifth Avenue to Amsterdam, is the slice of Manhattan known as Harlem. At the last census this section of New York City was home to 350,000 persons, but the number now is nearer a half-million. And since about 90 per cent of Harlem's population is colored, the place not only is the largest Negro community in the world but has lately become known as the Negro capital of the United States.

"Everybody talk about Harlem ain't goin' there," to modify the familiar spiritual, but large numbers are talking about Harlem these days. . . .

"Must-See" Harlem

Harlem remains on the "must" list of most New York visitors, partly because they are curious about Father Divine and his followers, but probably principally because they have read or heard something like the following:

"Harlem is different. It is the home of happy feet—gusty, swing-crazy, happy-go-lucky, wide open. Its laughter drowns you in mellow waves, nobody has a care big enough to blind a mosquito, and all kinds of thrills can be had with almost no searching."

This isn't exactly false—but it is a long way from being the truth. The description continues to be spread by three kinds of visitors: people whose faces are white, people whose pocketbooks never get dusty and people who don't know any better than to believe what they see.

To those who know better, to those who see Lennox Avenue between dawn and dusk, as well as between midnight and dawn, Harlem is "different" only because it underlines and emphasizes the Negro more vividly than any other community in the country; and because it splashes on a broad canvas, and with colorful strokes, the black man at his best and at his worst.

It has customs all its own, this city within a city. It has its own rewards and its own retributions. The wide publicity given its hot spots and hectic night life results from a deliberate whipping to a frenzy of its laughter, its dancing and its loving; but deep beneath the froth is a mass of faltering humans, sober-minded, unsung and inarticulate—though never without hope, never disloyal to the American way.

Thrilling Nightlife

Visitors, however, come looking for a thrill, and they are never disappointed. The following, for instance, is what might happen any night you decide to hail a cab, whirl through Central Park and up Seventh Avenue to watch the best of the swing artists in action—or, as Harlem might put it, "the hep cats lay their jive."

The Black Cat is your destination, and when you enter, swaying, squirming, gesticulating couples in an ecstasy of gin and passion are sending themselves out of this world. They pay you no mind. They are transfixed. They are practically unconscious.

You take a seat near the killer-dillers, dine, dance and drink and try to appear blasé—but in spite of yourself you are impressed. At the prices you wince, and rightly so; for the cost of everything doubled the moment your party filled the doorway.

Later you move on to an exotic studio, where weird rites from the Congo (by way of Beale Street) are performed. There is bedlam and foggy smoke, and you hesitate before slumping on a pillow and accepting a drink from a bronze goddess. Your eyes bulge at the antics you presently see.

"The real thing," some one behind you whispers. "Montmartre can't touch Harlem. * * * And if you think this is good you'd oughta go around the corner to the Witches Roost. It really comes on!"

So you go around the corner to the Witches Roost. You go around several other corners, eating golden fried chicken, made extra-special by a butter bath; you feast on chitterlings, pig snouts and gumbo—until you finally meet daylight face to face.

You duck in somewhere and gulp down coffee before returning downtown, bewildered and groggy. You have seen with your own eyes convincing evidences of the Negro's innocent, naive, laughter-loving nature. You are satisfied that when you hit New York again you will certainly look in at Harlem; and you urge your friends not to miss it for anything in the world.

Hard Truths

Well, it has to be said that little, if any, of what you saw was real. It was staged, as a Broadway show is staged. "Exposing" is Harlem's biggest and best-paying industry. The money that slumming parties spend night after night is a very welcome income for thousands of persons—but they work hard for it.

Most of the swaying couples in the Black Cat were merely going through a set routine and were listed on the expense sheet as "atmosphere." Those antics in the studios had been carefully rehearsed by youngsters to help pay family expenses or to earn money to bring members of their family from the South's cotton fields. And the man who tipped you off about the Witches Roost got his cut of the money you spent—for drumming up new business.

Harlem's other life is a thing apart. The only white people who see it are those who live there. It is a life involving the getting and holding of jobs; loving, marrying, sending children to school, keeping up social obligations, dying, and putting on a big show at the funeral. All of this amid congestion: by actual count one

Harlem block was found to contain 3,873 persons, or more than many a small American town.

In Harlem the rents are steep, the jobs far too few. The mortality rate is high, the crime rate very high. The New York Urban League reports a "vast army of young men and women who are unemployed." They are adrift, lolling about street corners, "no place to go, nothing to do."

A Resourceful Community

Yet life manages to go on, partly because Harlem folk are resourceful. A good portion of them keep a roof over their heads by giving parties. For the small sum of 10, 15 or 25 cents the Harlemite can attend a party any night in the week in somebody's apartment. It's a rent party. The host passes the hat in a congenial way and his dozens of guests donate the money he must hand over to the landlord in the morning.

Then there is always the chance—if an outside chance—to win at "numbers." This is not the $100,000,000-a-year racket it used to be in Harlem, but there are still thousands who ask each evening; with bated breath, "What came out today?" Despite the efforts of District Attorney Thomas E. Dewey, you can still put anything from a penny to $10 on the number you dreamed last night or saw on a passing truck. The lure of the numbers in Harlem is the same as in any other poverty-stricken group: a lucky gamble is the only chance ever to get the taste of riches.

Hardship, Loss, and Rebellion in the Corn Belt

Remley J. Glass

In 1930 approximately 123 million Americans lived on farms. Drought, economic failure, and dust storms caused tens of thousands of farmers to lose their land and homes during the Great Depression. Farmers who had borrowed money to buy machinery or land were unable to make payments. Nervous farmers sold their land at low prices while others fought back as best they could. In 1931 a Des Moines newspaper editor, trying to discourage the idea that all farmers were desperate to unload their farms, encouraged farmers to post signs on their land that read, "This farm is NOT for sale." Some farmers rebelled by threatening anyone attempting to buy a farm or by holding what were called "penny auctions" to disrupt the foreclosure process. In this article, lawyer Remley J. Glass describes how the Depression impacted the farming community where he lived.

Perhaps more than any other class, the country lawyers of the Corn Belt realize the present and the potential danger of the existing economic crisis as it affects the citizens of the farming areas of the Middle West and the country itself.

A city banker sees it as a question of liquidity of assets, security of deposits, or desirable loans; a professional economist views it as a maze of curves, most of them pointing downward, and a tempting opportunity to expound and perchance test his favorite theories; but the country lawyer gazes into troubled faces across his littered desk and listens to the concrete facts of foreclosed farms and lost homes, of bankruptcies and distraints for rent.

The banker and economist deal with figures and theories of recovery, but the country lawyer has to do with people suffering

Remley J. Glass, "Gentleman, the Corn Belt!" *Harper's Magazine*, vol. 167, June–November 1933, pp. 200–209.

loss not only of surplus and profits, but of homes and lifetime savings which they have held as security against sickness, old age, and death. It has ceased to be a question of sending the children to college or the purchase of an automobile and has become a struggle to pay taxes on the home and interest on the mortgage; to avoid tax sales and foreclosures; to keep a roof over the family, and to have the necessaries of life.

Sixty-odd years ago, after graduating from the State University and being admitted to the bar, my father came with his young wife to the little county seat where I was born. Here he continued in the practice of law until his death; and I now sit in the office where he sat for almost fifty years, gazing now and then, as he did, through the branches of the trees across the town square to the courthouse tower.

We have never been corporation lawyers; our clientele has come in the main from the sturdy agricultural citizenry of this formerly prosperous community. The fathers and grandfathers of present-day clients came to my father to have him prepare the deeds, examine the titles, and procure the loans when they settled here. The sons and grandsons of those pioneers now come to me and lay their troubles and worries and cares on my desk every day, and while I work over their problems, worries of the same sort regarding my own affairs are in the back of my mind.

My people were pioneer stock who settled in Iowa in 1855. My parents and grandparents were college bred and have contributed their share to the political and social life of the State. For eighty years the family has owned and operated farms in Iowa and, in the main, has gained its competency from the deep black soil of the Corn Belt. Therefore, my point of view is that of a professional man who, by inheritance, education, and experience is familiar with agricultural problems, and because of the investment of what is left of his own estate in farm lands, has a truly vital interest in this present crisis. . . .

The [1920s were] marked by a gradual decrease in the price of farm commodities, a shrinkage in farm values, and increasing attempts by the holders to collect second and third mortgages given during boom times. However, the foreclosure of a first or primary mortgage on Iowa real estate was as rare during this period as it had been in prior years. The basic value of Corn Belt land was still beyond question, and what few first-mortgage fore-closure actions were brought disturbed this confidence but little. During this same decade large drainage projects were inaugurated in the Corn Belt in order to bring large areas of "border" land under cultivation. Consolidated schools were erected to bring the highest type of educational facilities to the rural children. The proverbial little red schoolhouse became a modern brick building with enlarged faculties and increased facilities for education. Paved roads were built.

All these features had been demanded and are desirable; but the ability to pay for them has not continued. The general tax demands of school district, county, and State have equaled the interest on a thirty-dollar-per-acre mortgage over the entire State of Iowa; while special highway, drainage, and consolidated school assessments have increased the tax burden in areas affected by those improvements beyond bearing. For some years past, conservative mortgage lenders have hesitated to place loans on farms affected by these special levies, and in nearly every county the first of the flood of foreclosures was in such heavily taxed areas.

The drastic deflation of Iowa loans under orders from the Federal Reserve Board, upon which Smith Wildman Brookhart, depression Senator from Iowa, poured forth his venom, definitely marked the downward turn in the mythical prosperity of boom days. Despite our hopes for the better, conditions have grown steadily worse.

During the year after the great debacle of 1929 the flood of foreclosure actions did not reach any great peak, but in the years 1931 and 1932 the tidal wave was upon us. Insurance companies and large investors had not as yet realized (and in some instances do not yet realize) that, with the low price of farm commodities and the gradual exhaustion of savings and reserves, the formerly safe and sane investments in farm mortgages could not be worked out, taxes and interest could not be paid, and liquidation could not be made. With an utter disregard of the possibilities of payment or refinancing, the large loan companies plunged ahead to make the Iowa farmer pay his loans in full or turn over the real estate to the mortgage holder. Deficiency judgments and the resultant receiverships were the clubs they used to make the honest but indigent farm owners yield immediate possession of the farms.

Men who had sunk every dollar they possessed in the purchase, upkeep, and improvement of their home places were turned out with small amounts of personal property as their only assets. Landowners who had regarded farm land as the ultimate in safety, after using their outside resources in vain attempts to hold their lands, saw these assets go under the sheriff's hammer on the courthouse steps.

During the two-year period of 1931–32, in this formerly prosperous Iowa county, twelve and a half per cent of the farms went under the hammer, and almost twenty-five per cent of the mortgaged farm real estate was foreclosed. And the conditions in my home county have been substantially duplicated in every one of the ninety-nine counties of Iowa and in those of the surrounding States.

We lawyers of the Corn Belt have had to develop a new type of practice, for in pre-war days foreclosure litigation amounted to but a small part of the general practice. In these years of the depression almost one-third of the cases filed have to do with this situation. Our courts are clogged with such matters.

To one who for years has been a standpatter, both financially and politically, the gradual change to near-radicalism, both in himself and in those formerly conservative property owners for whom his firm has done business down the years, is almost incomprehensible, but none the less alarming. Friends and clients of years' standing have lost inherited competencies which had been increased by their own conservative management. Not only their profits, but their principal has been wiped out. The conservative investments in real estate which we Middle Westerners have for years considered the best possible have become not only not an asset, but a liability, with the possibility of deficiency judgments, that bane of mortgage debtors, staring us in the face. Not only have the luxuries and comforts of life been taken from us, but the necessaries are not secure.

Men and women who have lived industrious, comfortable, and contented lives have faced bravely the loss of luxuries and comforts, but there is a decided change in their attitude toward the financial and economic powers that be when conditions take away their homes and imperil the continued existence of their families.

The interests of insurance companies and outside corporations in Iowa real estate have resulted in a form of absentee ownership never before dreamed of. Large numbers of farms held by these outside interests are administered by men who do not have sympathetic appreciation of local conditions, and of the friendly relations which have been traditional between Corn Belt landlord and tenant.

The sympathetic, friendly inspection of the crops, the fences, and the live stock, which formed the Sunday afternoon diversion of the small landlord, has ceased. Now some young lad, clad like an English squire in riding boots and breeches, with a brief case and a Ford, drives up, hastily checks the acreage in corn and oats, inquires why the first payment of the cash rent has not been paid, tells the tenant that all checks for produce sold must be made out in the name of the company, and drives away. The personal element is gone.

Gone, too, is that pride of ownership which made possible the development of stock and dairy farms with their herds of fat cattle and hogs, their Jersey cows, their well-kept groves and buildings which beautified and developed the countryside. The former

Indignant farmers gather to discuss the fate of their farms and land. Some offered mob resistance to absentee owners.

owners were willing to use a large part of receipts from a farm's income to increase its value and appearance, but the present absentee owner regards it only as a source of possible dividends.

It used to be that a quarter section of farm land and a few shares of stock in the community bank marked a successful man; now it is too apt to have placed him in the bankruptcy court, after an harassing experience of foreclosures and suits brought by the receiver of the little country bank to collect the double assessment on his stock.

It is thought by many people that these sweeping changes affect only the land speculator but have no bearing on the individual farm owner who lived on and operated his farm. When conditions were favorable, when taxes were not too high and when there was no mortgage to meet, those men in the main have been able to meet the crisis by applying on the taxes and assessments the bulk of the earnings of the farm above their meager living. But this has been accomplished only by a sacrifice of upkeep of farm buildings and by loss of fertility in the farm itself. What we out in the Middle West term "hay wire" repairs have taken the place of necessary renewals of farm machinery. Live stock has been sold at ruinous prices. The future has been sacrificed to the exigent moment.

From a lawyer's point of view, one of the most serious effects of the economic crisis lies in the rapid and permanent disintegration of established estates throughout the Corn Belt. Families of moderate means as well as those of considerable fortunes who have been clients of my particular office for three or four generations in many instances have lost their savings, their investments, and their homes; while their business, which for many years has been a continuous source of income, has become merely an additional responsibility as we strive to protect them from foreclosures, judicial receivership, deficiency judgments, and probably bankruptcy.

Thank heaven, most country lawyers feel this responsibility to their old clients, and strive just as diligently to protect their clients' rights under present conditions as they did in the golden days before the depression. Every time, however, when I am called to defend a foreclosure action filed against some client or friend, it is forced on my mind that an estate accumulated through years of effort has not merely changed hands but has vanished into thin air.

As I sit here my mind turns to one after another of the prominent landowning families of this county who have lost their fortunes, not as a result of extravagance or carelessness, but because of conditions beyond their control, and which were not envisaged by the most farsighted. . . .

Take, if you please, what seems to me to have been a typical case of the tenant farmer, one Johannes Schmidt, a client of mine. . . .

In the year 1931 a drought in this part of the Corn Belt practically eliminated his crops, while what little he did raise was insufficient to pay his rent, and he went into 1932 with increased indebtedness for feed, back taxes, and back rent. While the crops in 1932 were wonderful and justified the statement that the Middle West is the market basket of the world, prices were so low as not to pay the cost of seed and labor in production without regard to taxes and rent.

Times were hard and the reverberations of October, 1929, had definitely reached the Corn Belt. The county-seat bank which held Johannes' paper was in hard shape. Much of its reserve had been invested in bonds recommended by Eastern bankers upon which default of interest and principal had occurred. When the bottom dropped out of the bond market the banking departments and examiners insisted upon immediate collection of slow farm loans, as liquidity was the watchword of bank examiners in the years 1929 to 1932. When Johannes sought to renew his bank loan, payment or else security on all his personal property was demanded without regard the needs of wife and family. Prices of farm products had fallen to almost nothing, oats were ten cents a bushel, corn twelve cents per bushel, while hogs, the chief cash crop in the Corn Belt, were selling at less than two and one half cents a pound. In the fall of 1932 a wagon load of oats would not pay for a pair of shoes; a truck load of hogs, which in other days would have paid all a tenant's cash rent, did not then pay the interest on a thousand dollars.

This man Schmidt had struggled and contrived as long as possible under the prodding of landlord and banker, and as a last resort came to see me about bankruptcy. We talked it over and with regret reached the conclusion it was the only road for him to take. He did not have even enough cash on hand to pay the thirty-dollar filing fee which I had to send to the Federal Court but finally borrowed it from his brother-in-law. The time of hearing came, and he and his wife and children sat before the Referee in Bankruptcy, while the Banker and the landlord struggled over priorities of liens and rights to crops and cattle. When the day was over this family went out from the office the owner of an old team of horses, a wagon, a couple of cows and five hogs, together with their few sticks of furniture and no place to go. . . .

I have represented bankrupt farmers and holders of claims for rent, notes, and mortgages against such farmers in dozens of bankruptcy hearings and court actions, and the most discouraging, disheartening experiences of my legal life have occurred when men of middle age, with families, go out of the bankruptcy court with furniture, team of horses and a wagon, and a little stock as all that is left from twenty-five years of work, to try once more—not to build up an estate—for that is usually impossible—but to provide clothing and food and shelter for the wife and children. And the powers that be seem to demand that these not only accept this situation but shall like it.

There is a growing feeling of bitterness in the Corn Belt. Many of us realize that economic pressure is forcing those who are forcing us but, nevertheless, a desire for retaliation has sprung into being in the past few years. Many men under economic pressure have come to feel that if nations and organizations of capital can disregard their obligations and their pledged word, the small farmer and business man should be granted similar privileges and similar immunities. . . .

After talking with dozens of the county officers, representatives of farm groups, and hundreds of farmers themselves from this section of Iowa, it seems to me to be the consensus of opinion that from ten to twenty-five per cent of the farm population are definitely radical, while as many more need only the urge of effective leadership and the power of mass psychology to be swung into the radical alignment. . . .

The closing of hundreds of banks, with the resultant impoverishment of many families and the forced collection of many capital loans to farmers, has resulted in a feeling of hostility toward the financial interests. Men who in normal times regarded their contractual obligations as sacred have not hesitated to repudiate their obligations when possible. When constituted authority, such as the courts and the officers of the law, were invoked to enforce the orders of the court, resistance and violence resulted.

In many sections of this and other States "penny sales" have been held at which a man's neighbors, by threats and force, have often reduced normal farm sale proceeds by almost one hundred per cent; milk and produce wars have been declared, during which all highways into a city have been guarded by rebellious farmers seeking to prevent other farmers from delivering these vital commodities until prices satisfactory to them were assured; and organized and successful attempts to force settlements by mortgage holders have resulted in a complete and definite abrogation of the power of the courts and constitutional authorities.

An instance in Boone County occurred where live stock and machinery worth over three thousand dollars brought less than thirty at one of the first of the "penny sales." The debtor's neighbors and friends first warned and then with blows drove off prospective bidders at this sale, bid in horses at twenty-five cents apiece, milk cows at a dime, and fat hogs at a nickel, and the next morning turned back their purchases to the former owner. Groups of farmers in many instances have intervened between mortgagor and mortgagee and between landlord and tenant to effect a settlement; and if such settlement was not made, crowds of hundreds at the judicial sales have exercised the power of public opinion and the power of their fists to carry out what they deemed fair. These unfortunately are not isolated instances but seem to be a definite part of the program of some of the farm organizations.

A year and a half ago mob resistance to a judicial sale first appeared in Iowa. The receiver of a small closed bank in Wright County sought to sell the mortgaged machinery and live stock of one of the bank's debtors. Indignant neighbors and friends stopped the sale and with violence drove the receiver and the sheriff from the farm. . . .

In Plymouth County, in April [1933], an organized group of hundreds of farmers defended one of their neighbors from rightful eviction in accordance with orders of court. Their resistance continued for a number of days. The sheriff and officers of the State Department of Justice were driven off the place; and the attorney, a college friend of mine who represented the owner of the property, was threatened with serious violence if he and his clients did not refrain from their lawful attempt to take possession of their own property.

When a lawyer friend of mine told me that an angry group of rural citizens from a nearby county had visited his office to demand the dismissal of a foreclosure action then pending, I suggested that he had better mail his instructions to the county sheriff and remain away from the scene lest in the morning paper there might appear a picture of the courthouse steps with an "X" marking the scene of the fatality. He went over to attend the sale in person and came back unharmed; but none of us knows when these threats may change to action.

The dead lion has his glories but the live dog has his comforts. I sincerely believe that, like my Scotch forefathers in Covenanter days, I could meet death for principle, but I am free to confess that when a few days ago a client of mine asked me to collect rent from a recalcitrant tenant I was mighty glad to effect a reasonably fair settlement for that client without having to face a milling mob of the angry neighbors and friends of that tenant.

Judges of our trial courts have been threatened and at last in an outburst of violence unprecedented in the Middle West a courtroom has been invaded by an organized mob and, because he refused to prostitute his office and violate his oath, a judge in one of the formerly prosperous counties of Iowa has been dragged from the bench, abducted, beaten, subjected to the gravest personal indignities, and hanged by the neck until he fainted from exhaustion. As I write, martial law has been declared in two Iowa counties by the Governor of Iowa, troops of the State have been sent to meet this heretofore unheard of condition, and military courts have been substituted for civil tribunals.

These things have happened in Iowa and the States of the Middle West, not in Latin America. Class-consciousness coupled with mob madness has definitely appeared in the Corn Belt.

Life in a Migrant Laborers' Camp

John Steinbeck

Since the early days of California agriculture, migrant laborers—farmworkers who travel from place to place seeking work—have been used to plant and harvest crops such as peaches, cotton, hops, and grapes for low pay. At the start of the twentieth century, a few dozen local laborers were sufficient to work a California farm's crops for most of a year, but up to two thousand laborers were needed for picking and packing a crop of peaches, for example, before the crop rotted. Prior to the 1930s, migrant workers had typically been made up of Mexican American or illegal immigrant populations.

In 1931 a drought that would last seven years began in the Midwest. Dust storms followed in 1932, eroding much of the dried farm soil and creating what is known as the Dust Bowl. Thousands of farm owners and workers from the Midwest lost their farms and jobs as a result and traveled west to become migrant laborers. Away from the comfort and modern amenities of their homes, such as plumbing and electricity, these farmers and their families set up temporary housing in what were called "squatters' camps" while they traveled around seeking work.

In the fall of 1936 John Steinbeck wrote a series of essays about the lives of these migrant laborers. Steinbeck's work helped bring their suffering to the public's attention—and also led to some controversy over whether concern for the living conditions of migrant workers had only been raised because the face of migrant labor was now white. The following piece, the second of seven essays Steinbeck published in the *San Francisco News* in October 1936, offers a glimpse at the everyday conditions of three typical migrant laborer families in a squatters' camp. Steinbeck won the Pulitzer Prize for his novel *The Grapes of Wrath* and received the Nobel Prize for Literature in 1968.

John Steinbeck, "The Harvest Gypsies," *San Francisco News*, October 6, 1936.

The squatters' camps are located all over California. Let us see what a typical one is like. It is located on the banks of a river, near an irrigation ditch or on a side road where a spring of water is available. From a distance it looks like a city dump, and well it may, for the city dumps are the sources for the material of which it is built. You can see a litter of dirty rags and scrap iron, of houses built of weeds, of flattened cans or of paper. It is only on close approach that it can be seen that these are homes.

The Upper Class

Here is a house built by a family who have tried to maintain a neatness. The house is about 10 feet by 10 feet, and it is built completely of corrugated paper. The roof is peaked, the walls are tacked to a wooden frame. The dirt floor is swept clean, and along the irrigation ditch or in the muddy river the wife of the family scrubs clothes without soap and tries to rinse out the mud in muddy water. The spirit of this family is not quite broken, for the children, three of them, still have clothes, and the family possesses three old quilts and a soggy, lumpy mattress. But the money so needed for food cannot be used for soap nor for clothes.

With the first rain the carefully built house will slop down into a brown, pulpy mush; in a few months the clothes will fray off the children's bodies while the lack of nourishing food will subject the whole family to pneumonia when the first cold comes.

Five years ago this family had fifty acres of land and a thousand dollars in the bank. The wife belonged to a sewing circle and the man was a member of the grange. They raised chickens, pigs, pigeons and vegetables and fruit for their own use; and their land produced the tall corn of the middle west. Now they have nothing.

If the husband hits every harvest without delay and works the maximum time, he may make four hundred dollars this year. But if anything happens, if his old car breaks down, if he is late and misses a harvest or two, he will have to feed his whole family on as little as one hundred and fifty.

But there is still pride in this family. Wherever they stop they try to put the children in school. It may be that the children will be in a school for as much as a month before they are moved to another locality.

Here, in the faces of the husband and his wife, you begin to see an expression you will notice on every face; not worry, but absolute terror of the starvation that crowds in against the borders of the camp. This man has tried to make a toilet by digging a hole in the ground near his paper house and surrounding it with an old piece of burlap. But he will only do things like that this year.

He is a newcomer and his spirit and decency and his sense of his own dignity have not been quite wiped out. Next year he will be like his next door neighbor.

The Middle Class

This is a family of six; a man, his wife and four children. They live in a tent the color of the ground. Rot has set in on the canvas so that the flaps and the sides hang in tatters and are held together with bits of rusty baling wire. There is one bed in the family and that is a big tick lying on the ground inside the tent.

They have one quilt and a piece of canvas for bedding. The sleeping arrangement is clever. Mother and father lie down together and two children lie between them. Then, heading the other way; the other two children lie, the littler ones. If the mother and father sleep with their legs spread wide, there is room for the legs of the children.

There is more filth here. The tent is full of flies clinging to the apple box that is the dinner table, buzzing about the foul clothes of the children, particularly the baby; who has not been bathed nor cleaned for several days.

This family has been on the road longer than the builder of the paper house. There is no toilet here, but there is a clump of willows nearby where human feces lie exposed to the flies—the same flies that are in the tent.

Two weeks ago there was another child, a four year old boy. For a few weeks they had noticed that he was kind of lackadaisical, that his eyes had been feverish.

They had given him the best place in the bed, between father and mother. But one night he went into convulsions and died, and the next morning the coroner's wagon took him away. It was one step down.

They know pretty well that it was a diet of fresh fruit, beans and little else that caused his death. He had no milk for months. With this death there came a change of mind in his family. The father and mother now feel that paralyzed dullness with which the mind protects itself against too much sorrow and too much pain.

And this father will not be able to make a maximum of four hundred dollars a year any more because he is no longer alert; he isn't quick at piece-work, and he is not able to fight clear of the dullness that has settled on him. His spirit is losing caste rapidly.

The dullness shows in the faces of this family, and in addition there is a sullenness that makes them taciturn. Sometimes they still start the older children off to school, but the ragged little things will not go; they hide in ditches or wander off by themselves until it is time to go back to the tent, because they are scorned in the school.

The better-dressed children shout and jeer, the teachers are quite often impatient with these additions to their duties, and the parents of the "nice" children do not want to have disease carriers in the schools.

The father of this family once had a little grocery store and his family lived in back of it so that even the children could wait on the counter. When the drought set in there was no trade for the store any more.

This is the middle class of the squatters' camp. In a few months this family will slip down to the lower class.

Dignity is all gone, and spirit has turned to sullen anger before it dies.

The Lower Class

The next door neighbor family of man, wife and three children of from three to nine years of age, have built a house by driving willow branches into the ground and wattling weeds, tin, old paper and strips of carpet against them.

A few branches are placed over the top to keep out the noonday sun. it would not turn water at all. There is no bed.

Somewhere the family has found a big piece of old carpet. It is on the ground. To go to bed the members of the family lie on the ground and fold the carpet up over them.

The three year old child has a gunny sack tied about his middle for clothing. He has the swollen belly caused by malnutrition.

He sits on the ground in the sun in front of the house, and the little black fruit flies buzz in circles and land on his closed eyes and crawl up his nose until he weakly brushes them away.

They try to get at the mucous in the eye-corners. This child seems to have the reactions of a baby much younger. The first year he had a little milk, but he has had none since.

He will die in a very short time. The older children may survive. Four nights ago the mother had a baby in the tent, on the dirty carpet. It was born dead, which was just as well because she could not have fed it at the breast; her own diet will not produce milk.

After it was born and she had seen that it was dead, the mother rolled over and lay still for two days. She is up today, tottering around. The last baby, born less than a year ago, lived a week. This woman's eyes have the glazed, far-away look of a sleep walker's eyes.

She does not wash clothes any more. The drive that makes for cleanliness has been drained out of her and she hasn't the energy. The husband was a share-cropper once, but he couldn't make it go. Now he has lost even the desire to talk.

He will not look directly at you for that requires will, and will needs strength. He is a bad field worker for the same reason. It takes him a long time to make up his mind, so he is always late in moving and late in arriving in the fields. His top wage, when he can find work now; which isn't often, is a dollar a day.

The children do not even go to the willow clump any more. They squat where they are and kick a little dirt. The father is vaguely aware that there is a culture of hookworm in the mud along the river bank. He knows the children will get it on their bare feet.

But he hasn't the will nor the energy to resist. Too many things have happened to him. This is the lower class of the camp.

This is what the man in the tent will be in six months; what the man in the paper house with its peaked roof will be in a year, after his house has washed down and his children have sickened or died, after the loss of dignity and spirit have cut him down to a kind of sub-humanity.

Nowhere to Turn for Help

Helpful strangers are not well-received in this camp. The local sheriff makes a raid now and then for a wanted man, and if there is labor trouble the vigilantes may burn the poor houses. Social workers, survey workers have taken case histories.

They are filed and open for inspection. These families have been questioned over and over about their origins, number of children living and dead.

The information is taken down and filed. That is that. It has been done so often and so little has come of it.

And there is another way for them to get attention. Let an epidemic break out, say typhoid or scarlet fever, and the country doctor will come to the camp and hurry the infected cases to the pest house. But malnutrition is not infectious, nor is dysentery, which is almost the rule among the children.

The county hospital has no room for measles, mumps, whooping cough; and yet these are often deadly to hunger-weakened children. And although we hear much about the free clinics for the poor, these people do not know how to get the aid and they do not get it. Also, since most of their dealings with authority are painful to them, they prefer not to take the chance.

This is the squatters' camp. Some are a little better, some much worse. I have described three typical families. In some of the camps there are as many as three hundred families like these. Some are so far from water that it must be bought at five cents a bucket.

And if these men steal, if there is developing among them a suspicion and hatred of well-dressed, satisfied people, the reason is not to be sought in their origin nor in any tendency to weakness in their character.

The Apple Vendors and Unemployed of New York City

Frances D. McMullen

While Wall Street crashed and the Depression began, the states of Oregon and Washington had unusually successful apple crops. In 1930 the International Apple Shippers' Association decided that one way to handle the surplus would be to have the unemployed sell the apples on the streets. The jobless would receive a crate of apples and sell them for five cents apiece; after paying off the cost of the crate, the profits were theirs to keep. Early in the Depression, before there was any federal aid, communities were encouraged to look after their own people, and sympathetic passersby bought the apples in droves. However, before long the apple selling became problematic. The sheer numbers of apple sellers—six thousand in New York City by the fall of 1930—meant they were on nearly every corner. Complaints of apple sellers blocking doorways and rotting fruit littering the streets led to public disfavor. By April 1931 police had banned the apple sellers from many parts of Manhattan. Eventually, they disappeared altogether.

The following article by *New York Times* staff writer Frances D. McMullen appeared in January 1931. It recalls the early days of the apple vendors in New York City and describes a sympathetic and charitable city—not just to the apple vendors but to all of the unemployed.

It was a bitter day. The shopping crowd on Fifth Avenue hunched down in the thick of its fur collars and hurried along. Parts of it dropped off quickly through the doors of store fronts, which swung again to emit new currents that joined the main stream hesitantly, pausing first to gather courage for the plunge into the cold. In the surging throngs none tarried to look about; all ducked and scurried to a shelter as soon as possible.

Help the Unemployed—Buy an Apple

A man stood on a bleak and busy corner. He had no overcoat— and the wind howled. Beside him, a box of apples. At times his red hands mechanically polished the already glossy fruit; at times they went into his inadequate pockets; then motion was trans- ferred to feet, slowly stamping, and lips that chanted: "Help the unemployed, Buy an apple."

Business was poor. Who cared to put chattering teeth into fruit that was sure to be cold no matter what glow numb fingers might have rubbed into its fiery skin? Who cared to tuck a bag of apples beneath a rigid arm? The passing world was bent on getting its errands done and keeping warm. Then the apple man saw a signal. The stream of vehicles moving haltingly through the avenue had come to a halt before a red traffic light. A bus driver beckoned. With a couple of apples, the man threaded his way through the jam of vehicles. Now the light flashed green again. Trucks and taxis snorted to go. The bus began to roll. There was yet time, but the bus driver made no motion pocket-ward. Instead, he peeled off his gloves, thrust them into the bare hand of the apple man and moved along.

Sympathetic New Yorkers

Wherever apple men place themselves—and they prefer a stand where people pass—some act of solicitude is sure to show itself to any one who loiters long enough; for since the apple has be- come the sign of unemployment the public has come to regard the vendors as people who need a helping hand. As a fashion has been set for New Yorkers to eat apples on the street, so has an- other—to engage in sidewalk philanthropy that is more akin to fellowship than to charity.

In the centre of the shopping district an apple man, young, slight, evidently "white collar," buttons the coat of his neat blue suit over a lightweight sweater and coughs. A woman pauses, an elderly, motherly looking woman with a sad expression in her eyes.

"I'll take an apple," she says, and from her purse digs out a quarter. She pauses a moment, inquires if the young man has a bag, decides to take five apples, lingers a moment more, starts on dubiously and turns back.

"Son, where's your overcoat?" she inquires.

He mumbles something with an embarrassed gesture. She drops her voice in reply. The stand is entrusted for the time being to the apple man next door, and the young man and the woman walk off. He returns alone, in a new overcoat, and explains to his curbstone neighbor. "What do you know? Bought it for me. Said she had a boy once."

An apple man in the rain standing gingerly on a piece of corrugated board.

"Takes some shoes for this," a customer jovially remarks, with the serious afterthought, "How're yours, old man? Pretty thin? Here, go over there and get them soled. I'll watch your stand."

An apple man on a snowy afternoon dejectedly sitting on an empty box with a fireplug for support. A young woman, bundle-laden from the opposite store, pauses as she enters her parked car and turns to the vendor. "How'd you like half a day off? Let me have the rest of your box."

A well-dressed woman before an apple man, obviously wishing to buy but looking around to see what she could do with an apple. A sandwich man, lean and wistful between his placards. She buys the apple, offers it to the sandwich man. He gratefully accepts.

A cripple on a Houston Street corner. An automobile stops. A well-dressed man gets out with a box of apples. "Here's your stock, old man. Let us know when you run short. Some one from the office will go by the store and get you another."

The Poor Help the Poor

At Sixth Avenue and Forty-second Street an apple stand momentarily deserted by its vendor. A lunch-going crowd rushing for the traffic break upsets the neat pile without stopping to look back. A hatless girl in a sweater out on an errand, stops, picks up the apples and arranges the stand in order. A weary apple woman sits on a box apparently too exhausted to rise and serve two customers pausing at her stand. A neighboring dealer comes over, completes the sale and drops two nickels into her cup. A genial cripple, peddling shoestrings and pencils, wheels himself up to an apple stand, nickel in hand, and makes his choice. The apple man waves his nickel aside with a smile.

Down beside the river among the stores where the apples come from, a bent man struggles toward the subway under the load of an unopened box. A truck, despite its windshield notice— "No riders"—pulls up at the curb. "Give you a lift, Mister?"

Generosity for the Unemployed

It is noontime and a crowd pours out of the building which houses the municipal employment agency. The job hunters come out ostensibly for lunch. Some stroll off, but many will regale themselves only with a breath of air and the slight warmth of the pale Winter sun. A group of half a dozen lean dejectedly against the wall, watching the automobiles go by. Many cars pass up and down Lafayette Street, some high-powered and shiny and carrying each a lone bulky figure on the back seat, toward luncheon conferences doubtless no less high-powered and shiny. One of these stops. The chauffeur calls to the group: "Hey, you fellows, mind stepping over here a minute?"

The occupant of the back seat deals out half dollars all around, and the bidding, "Go and get yourself some lunch."

In the job line-up in the chill, dim early morning, some one slumps against the wall and slips weakly down. A policeman bends over him, "What's the trouble, buddy?" There is a mention of food. The policeman fumbles in his pocket, slips a few coins into the bony hand, "Go get yourself something to eat; you'll feel better then."

On Rivington Street a woman comes out of a lodging house— an elderly withered person with traces of beauty and the hint of former grace. A middle-aged policeman stops her for a chat and presses a tiny wad into her palm, "Pay your rent a couple weeks, maybe."

The Bowery. A man stands at the Salvation Army food depot, shivering beneath his light coat. Along comes a red-headed youth warmly buttoned in an army overcoat; he takes it off, throws it around the other's shoulders, thrust his hands into his pockets and goes his way whistling before the other can speak.

Outside the Bowery Mission three men stand in the sun. They

talk spasmodically. A young man, happy-go-lucky, fresh-looking, as if recently from the farm, joins them, brandishing a pair of dollar bills.

"Had a job yesterday," he announces triumphantly. "How about coming along for a feed?"

East of the Bowery, where city slum clearance plans have cut a wide swath through solid blocks of old tenements and left a strip of littered ground, fires made of old boxes and bits of wreckage burn here and there. Sometimes they can scarcely be seen for the huddled humanity that stretches its hands toward the blaze. But let a newcomer arrive and room is invariably made for him. They have all come from the near-by soup kitchen or are about to join its line

Eating: An Inalienable Right

A group of a dozen men, some of whom grew up in the neighborhood, are having their luncheon in a restaurant that overlooks the vacant ground. There is talk, the sum of which is that eating is one of the inalienable rights of man. They decide they will make good this right for others who eye them hungrily from outside. They pool their money, obtain permission to use the city's plot, and plan to build a kitchen and mess shack in memory of a departed comrade. From the line that forms before the shack they will choose men to do the chores in return for three meals a day, a bunk and a bath once a week. They find a bakery that will give bread and an electric ice box company that will supply packing cases for fuel. The kitchen is opened. Food steams in a 300-gallon pot. Men wait and are fed. At the head of the line stands one of the dozen to greet the guests and pass out spoons.

Chronology

1928

October: In New York during the national presidential campaign, Republican candidate Herbert Hoover delivers his "rugged individualism" speech, reemphasizing traditional American values such as self-reliance and insisting that the federal government play a minimal role in people's lives.

November: Hoover is elected president, defeating his Democratic opponent, Alfred E. Smith, by a wide margin.

1929

October: The New York stock market crashes, sending the U.S. economy into a disastrous tailspin; in the following two years the nation sinks into a severe economic depression; the rest of the industrialized world quickly follows suit.

1930

December: The once-powerful Bank of the United States, along with many other smaller banks, fails; 4.5 million Americans are now unemployed.

1931

April: As the Great Depression tightens its grip, automobile tycoon Henry Ford lays off seventy-five thousand workers.

1932

January: President Hoover signs into law the Reconstruction Finance Corporation, designed to help put banks and large businesses back on their feet.

July: Franklin D. Roosevelt, governor of New York State, wins the Democratic presidential nomination for the upcoming election.

September: Roosevelt delivers his "Commonwealth Club" speech, in which he asserts that government owes every citizen a right to life and a measure of security and happiness.

November: Roosevelt defeats Hoover in a landslide, winning the electoral vote by a margin of 472 to 59.

1933

March: U.S. unemployment reaches a devastating 15 million; Roosevelt is inaugurated as the thirty-second president; in his stirring inaugural address, he tells his countrymen that "the only thing we have to fear is fear itself"; the president shuts down U.S. banks and orders that their books be examined; Roosevelt gives his first radio "Fireside Chat"; the president submits to Congress the Agricultural Adjustment Act and the Civilian Conservation Corps, launching the massive legislative assault on the Depression known thereafter as the New Deal.
May: Congress passes the Federal Emergency Relief Act, Emergency Farm Mortgage Act, Truth-in-Securities Act, and the Tennessee Valley Authority Act, the last of these designed to reshape the water system of the Tennessee River Valley and to provide cheap electricity for millions of Americans.
June: Congress passes Roosevelt's National Industrial Recovery Act and Home Owner's Loan Act.
December: The Eighteenth Amendment to the Constitution, prohibiting the sale of alcoholic beverages, is repealed.

1934

June: Roosevelt signs into law the Securities Exchange Act, which initiates federal regulation of trading practices.
July: The Federal Communications Commission is created, providing for federal regulation of radio, telegraph, and cable businesses; Congress passes the National Housing Act.

1935

April: Roosevelt creates the Resettlement Administration, designed to deal with the severe problems of rural poverty.
August: Congress passes the Wealth Tax Act, providing for higher taxes on well-to-do Americans; the president signs the Social Security Act, creating a national old-age pension system.
September: Louisiana's governor, Huey Long, who had proposed a widely popular wealth redistribution program ("Share the Wealth"), is assassinated in Baton Rouge.

1936

February: The Supreme Court declares the Agricultural Adjustment Act unconstitutional.

November: Roosevelt is reelected, defeating his Republican opponent, Kansas governor Alf Landon, by a crushing electoral margin of 523 to 8.

1937

April: The American economy finally reaches the level of output it had maintained in 1929 before the beginning of the Depression.

May: The Supreme Court upholds the constitutionality of the Social Security Act.

August: With recovery seemingly taking hold, the nation experiences a sudden recession (economic downturn).

1938

June: Congress authorizes billions of dollars for new public works projects to fight the effects of the recent recession; Congress passes the Fair Labor Standards Act, providing for a minimum wage of forty cents an hour and a forty-hour workweek.

1939

September: Raymond Moley, formerly one of Roosevelt's closest advisers, publishes his book, *After Seven Years*, in which he severely criticizes the president and the New Deal; war erupts in Europe as Germany, led by Nazi dictator Adolf Hitler, invades Poland.

1941–1945

The United States fights in World War II against Germany, Italy, and Japan; a virtual avalanche of American war production helps to pull the nation the rest of the way out of the Depression.

1945

April: Franklin D. Roosevelt, architect of the New Deal and principal victor of World War II, dies at the age of sixty-three in the midst of his fourth term as president; he is succeeded by Harry S. Truman.

For Further Research

Books

Edward Behr, *Prohibition: Thirteen Years That Changed America.* New York: Arcade, 1996.

Ben S. Bernanke, *Essays on the Great Depression.* New Jersey: Princeton University Press, 2000.

Ted Conover, *Rolling Nowhere: Riding the Rails with America's Hoboes (Vintage Departures).* New York: Vintage, 2001.

Spencer Crew (introduction), Cynthia Goodman and Henry Louis Gates Jr. (foreword), *Unchained Memories: Readings from the Slave Narratives.* New York: Bulfinch Press, 2003.

Edward Robb Ellis, *A Nation in Torment: The Great American Depression, 1929–1939.* New York: Kodansha America, 1995.

David Emblidge and Marcy Ross, eds., *My Day: The Best of Eleanor Roosevelt's Acclaimed Newspaper Columns, 1936–1962.* Cambridge, MA: De Capo Press, 2001.

Albert Fried, *FDR and His Enemies.* New York: St. Martin's Press, 1999.

David M. Kennedy, *Freedom from Fear: The American People in Depression and War, 1929–1945.* New York: Oxford University Press, 1999.

William E. Leuchtenburg, *Franklin D. Roosevelt and the New Deal.* New York: Perennial, 1963.

Karal Ann Marling, *Wall-to-Wall America: Post-Office Murals in the Great Depression.* Minneapolis: University of Minnesota Press, 2000.

Robert S. McElvaine, *The Depression and New Deal: A History in Documents (Pages from History).* New York: Oxford University Press, 2000.

———, *The Great Depression: America 1929–1941.* New York: Times Books, 1984.

George H. Nash, *Life of Herbert Hoover: The Humanitarian, 1914–1917.* New York: W.W. Norton, 1988.

Dennis Nishi, ed., *The Great Depression*. San Diego: Greenhaven Press, 2001.

Eleanor Roosevelt, *The Autobiography of Eleanor Roosevelt*. Cambridge, MA: De Capo Press, 2000.

Robert Sobel, *Panic on Wall Street: A History of America's Financial Disasters*. Toronto: Collier-Macmillan Canada, 1969.

John Steinbeck, *The Grapes of Wrath*. New York: Alfred A. Knopf, 1993.

Studs Terkel, *Hard Times: An Oral History of the Great Depression*. New York: The New Press, 2000.

T.H. Watkins, *The Great Depression: America in the 1930s*. Boston: Little, Brown, 1993.

Donald Worster, *Dust Bowl: The Southern Plains in the 1930s*. New York: Oxford University Press, 1982.

Web Sites

Photographs from the Farm Security Administration–Office of War Information Collection, 1935–1945, are found at the Prints and Photographs Division, Library of Congress: http://memory.loc.gov/ammem/fsowhome.html.

A collection of documents and photographs for further research is found at http://newdeal.feri.org.

A page of Great Depression research and information links is found at http://americanhistory.about.com/cs/greatdepression.

An overview of cultural history during the Depression years is found at www.geocities.com/bettye_sutton/greatdepression.html.

Information on the Works Progress Administration (WPA) arts projects and links to state-specific information, WPA exhibits, and other WPA information sites are found at www.wpamurals.com.

Index